ACKNOWLEDGEMENTS

This publication would not have been possible without the wealth of information discovered while on this title-winning footballing journey. Also, it is important to state that certain statistics and details are not universally agreed upon. In such instances I have used my best judgement, but then, this book is primarily a celebration of an exceptional season in the history of Ipswich Town Football Club and aims to excite and inspire Town fans of all ages, and in the case of some, bring some great memories and emotions flooding back.

I wish to express my thanks to Elizabeth Edwards and Colin Kreidewolf for their help and acknowledge the following sources, all of which I have referred to in varying degrees:

www.prideofanglia.com
Ipswich Town, Champions 1961/62, by Martin Brooks.
The Men Who Made the Town by John Eastwood and Tony Moyse.
Ipswich Town FC - the 1960s, from Ramsey to Robson by Terry Hunt.
Suffolk Punch, Ipswich Town FC 1936-96, edited by Tony Moyse.
Ipswich Town Top Team 1961.62, East Anglian Daily Times.
The Curse of the Jungle Boy, Ray Crawford.

A big thank you to you all! Dedicated to all Town fans, past, present and future.

FIRST DIVISION 1961/62
CHAMPIONS

Written by Brian Leng
Statistics compiled by Chris Leng

a twocan publication

UP THE TOWN!

When Alf Ramsey was appointed manager of Ipswich Town during the 1955 close season, no one could have possibly predicted the incredible events in the years that followed as the new man at the helm led the small Suffolk club to the very pinnacle of the national game and would eventually go on to be widely acknowledged as English football's greatest-ever manager.

Amazingly, Ramsey had no previous managerial experience when the Ipswich board took the brave decision to offer him the Portman Road hot-seat vacated by Scott Duncan. Nevertheless, as a player he had enjoyed a highly impressive career as a full-back, first with Southampton and then Tottenham Hotspur where he won a League Championship medal in 1950/51. Ramsey also won 32 caps for his country including the ill-fated 1950 World Cup in Brazil when rank outsiders USA inflicted a humiliating 1-0 defeat over England that shocked the football world.

Perhaps more importantly however, he was also a member of the England team that was defeated 6-3 by Hungary at Wembley in 1953, the first continental team to ever triumph on English soil. Ramsey actually netted a penalty that day, but that would no doubt have been small consolation given the manner of England's defeat which was simply reinforced when they were hammered 7-1 in the return fixture in Budapest.

The results sent shock waves through the English game and for the national side, regarded for so long as the kings of world football, the tide was clearly turning and it soon became abundantly clear that unless radical changes were introduced, they would soon become a second class football nation. The man who would pioneer those changes and ultimately lead England back to the very top of world football in 1966 was Alf Ramsey, but first came arguably an even greater achievement in the infinitely more humble surroundings of Portman Road.

When Town's new boss arrived at Ipswich in August 1955, he found a club where morale was rock bottom following their relegation the previous season after surviving only one campaign in Division Two, though he spoke in positive terms when he addressed fans in the supporter's association handbook:

'May I begin by saying "Pleased to meet you" and I sincerely hope that our association will be a happy and successful one. In the past you have supported the club 100% and I would like to feel that in this, my first year as manager, you will do the same. May our slogan, as Mr. Scott Duncan has said in previous years, still be "Up the Town!"'

For his first season in charge, Ramsey was happy to give the previous season's first-team players the chance to impress, but one new face to arrive was Jimmy Leadbetter who had been signed from Brighton and Hove Albion by Scott Duncan shortly before he became Secretary of the club. Few could have envisaged that the spindly-legged Scottish winger would turn out to be such a significant figure throughout Alf Ramsey's time at Portman Road.

The new Ipswich Town boss also inherited one or two other players who would soon become key men in the years ahead, including wing-half John Elsworthy and centre-forward Ted Phillips who had become something of a forgotten man at Portman Road and had actually been loaned out to Eastern Counties League side Stowmarket a month before Ramsey's arrival, for the duration of the 1955/56 season.

After a slow start, Town finished the 1955/56 campaign strongly and were desperately unlucky not to clinch promotion back to Division Two, finishing just one point behind second-placed Brighton and Hove Albion. However, the campaign did see two significant arrivals at Portman Road with goalkeeper Roy Bailey joining from Crystal Palace and full-back Larry Carberry signing amateur terms. Both were to become key members of Ramsey's revolutionary side and both would give the club sterling service in the years ahead.

Having come so close, hopes were high for the 1956/57 season, yet Ramsey's men got off to a dreadful start to the campaign winning only one of there first nine games to find themselves rooted at the foot of the table. However, on a more positive note, Ramsey had brought in Ted Phillips to lead the Town attack and he exploded onto the scene, spearheading a remarkable revival that saw his team quickly climb the table.

Phillips netted an amazing 41 league goals, the highest in the entire Football League, in a marvellous campaign that saw Ipswich clinch the Division Three South title and promotion back to the second tier.

The following three seasons saw Town consolidate their position in Division Two as Ramsey continued to strengthen his squad with shrewd acquisitions. There were no established names or star players arriving at Portman Road, just unknown journeymen who had spent most of their careers in the lower leagues, probably never dreaming that they might soon be picking up League Championship winners medals.

Key signings to arrive during this period included Andy Nelson, a solid central-defender who was signed from West Ham United for a then club record fee of £8,500 and who would eventually take over as club captain. John Compton from Chelsea, and winger Roy Stephenson from Leicester City both arrived in July 1960.

TED PHILLIPS IN DIVISION TWO
ACTION AT THE VALLEY,
CHARLTON ATHLETIC 1-3 IPSWICH TOWN,
16 APRIL 1960

Defender Bill Baxter, a man who would go on to become something of a legend at Portman Road and make over 450 appearances for the club, arrived in June 1960. However, it was the signing of centre-forward Ray Crawford, a £5,000 capture from Portsmouth that would have by far the most significant impact. Teaming up with Ted Phillips, the pair quickly developed into arguably the most lethal strike partnership in the game with Crawford eventually winning full international honours for England.

All of these bargain-basement players and more were gradually moulded into a new-look Ipswich Town team playing an exciting brand of attacking football, the like of which had never been witnessed previously at Portman Road. Suddenly, Town began to look likely candidates for promotion to Division One and as the 1959/60 season drew to a close the were sitting in fourth place, but a disappointing return of only three points from the final seven games saw them finish the campaign in eleventh place.

Nevertheless, the season did see the emergence of Ted Phillips and Ray Crawford as the pair netted 43 league and cup goals with Phillips in particular beginning to attract the attention of one or two top clubs. Fulham were the first to show their hand then Liverpool tabled a bid for the man whose career seemed to be heading nowhere only a couple of years previously. Fortunately for Town, these offers were both rebuffed by the Ipswich board, no doubt on the advice of Alf Ramsey who always insisted he had come to Ipswich to build a team and not sell his star players.

The decision to hang onto Phillips would bear rich reward the following season when Ramsey's team took the Second Division by storm to clinch the championship and promotion to the top flight. A truly brilliant campaign of devastating attacking football saw Town net 100 goals, 40 of which were scored by Crawford, who was top scorer, and Phillips who bagged 30.

At the time the pair were the most prolific strike partnership in the English game although as Ted Phillips later recalled, he owed everything to Alf Ramsey: "I would have been nothing without Alf, he made me when he took over at Ipswich. He was a god to me. I was better for just talking to Alf, never mind how he put me right in training. He chatted to me and built up my confidence. He taught me when to run and when I went through the middle, the likes of Jimmy Leadbetter, Roy Stephenson and big John Elsworthy would thread the ball through. I just went 'bang' and hit it as hard as I could. If it didn't make the net and the 'keeper got his hands to it, Ray Crawford would invariably follow up and get the rebound."

When Town began to emerge as front runners for promotion the tabloid press began to label them a 'Cinderella club' and when the title was secured, chairman John Cobbold had the perfect response when he commented: 'Cinderella's getting quite a big girl now, isn't she!' Nevertheless, few people outside of Ipswich gave Town any chance of survival in the top flight particularly when their team strengthening was restricted to one major signing in the transfer market, inside-forward Doug Moran who was acquired for a modest £12,000 from Falkirk.

Predictably, the bookies immediately installed Ramsey's team as favourites for relegation and their odds for lifting the league title were set at a staggering 500/1.

Understandably perhaps, Town's success in lifting the Second Division title was widely regarded by the press as little more than a flash in the pan, particularly bearing in mind that it was achieved with a squad of unknown players, most of whom had spent their entire careers in the lower leagues. What the media had not recognised however was the team ethic and new tactical approach and team spirit that Alf Ramsey had instilled in his team and perhaps more importantly, his ability to get the very best out of each and every player in his squad.

Jimmy Leadbetter later recalled: "Alf was a lovely man. He treated me like a man, not as a daft wee laddie, and he gained my total respect. He got it from all the players. Personally, I cannot talk too highly of him. He would never put people in an awkward position. If he had anything to say he would just have a wee blether in the corner. None of this shouting at the top of his voice like some of the big-mouths who are managers today and seem to enjoy belittling their players. When England sacked Alf they made a big mistake, he could have continued to do a good job for many more years."

Left-winger Leadbetter and Roy Stephenson on the opposite flank were fundamental to Ramsey's plans and were employed in an entirely different manner to traditional wide men of the 1950s whose job was to race down to the bye-line and whip in crosses for the oncoming forwards.

Instead, Leadbetter and Stephenson were played much deeper, even taking on defensive duties when required, and when in possession, they were instructed to fire diagonal crosses into the opposition penalty area as soon as possible. The ploy had worked to devastating effect in Division Two but the question was, how would Town fair when they came up against the really big guns in the English game.

Even Alf Ramsey himself acknowledged that the challenge facing his side was huge, stating to supporters:

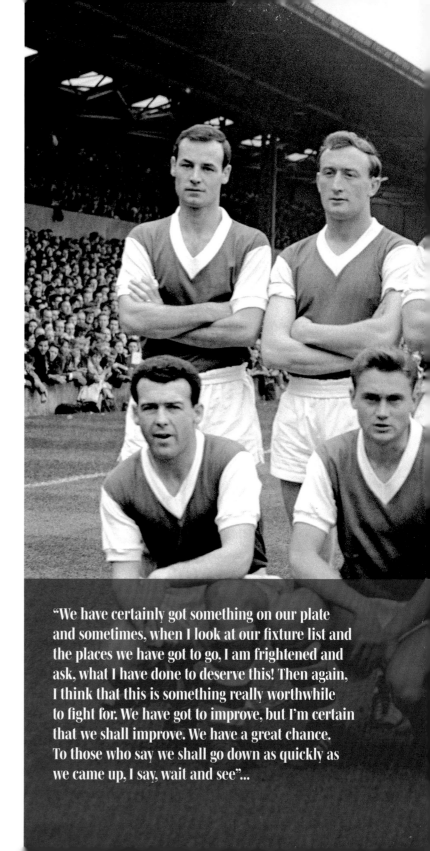

"We have certainly got something on our plate and sometimes, when I look at our fixture list and the places we have got to go, I am frightened and ask, what I have done to deserve this! Then again, I think that this is something really worthwhile to fight for. We have got to improve, but I'm certain that we shall improve. We have a great chance. To those who say we shall go down as quickly as we came up, I say, wait and see"...

"I THINK WE SHALL SHOW PEOPLE WE ARE QUITE A TEAM."

9

IPSWICH TOWN'S FIRST DIVISION ONE FIXTURE AT BOLTON WANDERERS

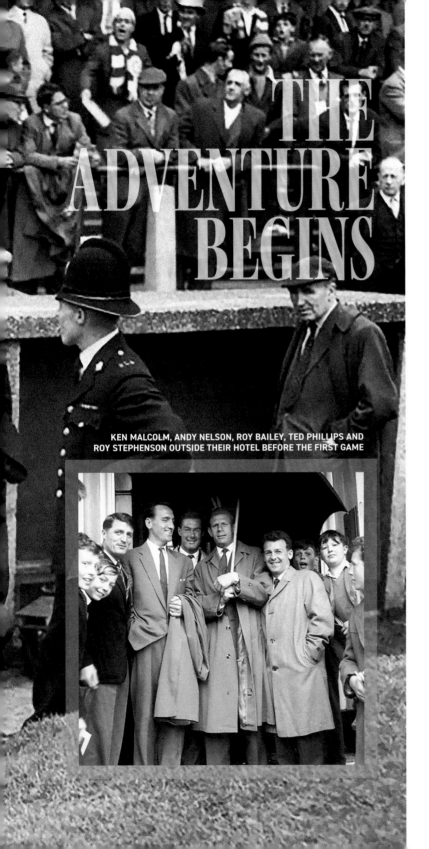

THE ADVENTURE BEGINS

KEN MALCOLM, ANDY NELSON, ROY BAILEY, TED PHILLIPS AND ROY STEPHENSON OUTSIDE THEIR HOTEL BEFORE THE FIRST GAME

The fixtures certainly did Ipswich no favours with their first two games being away from home. Both were up in Lancashire, so Ramsey and his squad set up their base in The Queen's hotel in the centre of Manchester, and the Ipswich Town boss had also managed to acquire the use of Manchester United's training ground at 'The Cliff'.

Their first-ever game in the top flight, ironically their 700th Football League game, was against Bolton Wanderers at Burnden Park and a few days later they headed up to Turf Moor to face Burnley, one of the top sides of the day.

Bolton had flirted with relegation the previous season, but were still a formidable opponent, rarely conceding goals at Burnden Park. Alf Ramsey fielded virtually all of the players who had helped clinch the Second Division title with the exception of Doug Moran who was making his Town debut following his £12,000 move from Falkirk.

The game quickly developed into a dour encounter with Ipswich creating the best opportunities with Leadbetter and Crawford both guilty of missing gilt-edged chances with the goal at their mercy. Baxter, playing in an attacking wing-half role came closest to scoring when Wanderers 'keeper Eddie Hopkinson tipped a great shot onto the post. Other than that there was little goalmouth action although on the hour mark, McAdams had the ball in the net for the home side only to see his effort ruled out for a foul on Nelson.

This was an extremely satisfactory result for Town's first encounter in Division One where they more than matched their vastly experienced opponents and were well worth their share of the spoils.

If Town's Burnden Park encounter had been something of a damp squib in terms of entertainment, their game against Burnley a few days later could hardly have been more of a contrast as both teams served up a real feast of brilliant attacking football.

As early as the fourth minute, Phillips rattled the woodwork with a powerful drive, but it was Burnley that opened the scoring through Pointer midway through the first-half. The home side's lead lasted fifteen minutes before Phillips became the first Ipswich player to score in the top flight, heading home from Leadbetter's precise cross. Soon afterwards however, the Town striker turned villain when he lost possession allowing Harris to race clear and slot the ball past Bailey.

The second half continued in the same vein and after only seven minutes Crawford levelled the scores only for Town to fall behind again when Miller headed home Connelly's cross.

With fifteen minutes remaining Phillips looked to have earned Ipswich the point their play had richly deserved when his shot was deflected past Blacklaw, but the home side clinched the win when McIlroy netted following a mix-up between Bailey and Carberry.

Despite the defeat Ramsey was delighted with his team's performance saying: "It is the best performance I have seen from any Ipswich team since I have been connected with the club. It was a wonderful match in which the football rose to a very high standard

There was a huge air of expectation among Ipswich Town fans as they awaited Portman Road's first-ever game in Division One and all seat tickets were sold well in advance of the fixture against Manchester City. Sadly, there would be no celebrations as Ramsey's team were beaten by a powerful City side although they had looked the better side for most of the game only to concede two late goals to give the visitors a 4-2 victory. To add to their disappointment, Ken Malcolm sustained a knee injury which, together with a long bout of sciatica, kept the Town full-back out for the rest of the campaign.

Only one point from three games saw Ramsey's team sink to the lower reaches of the league that predictably, had the profits of doom circling over Portman Road.

DIVISION ONE

	31 AUGUST 1961	P	W	D	L	F	A	GA	P
1	Manchester City	4	4	0	0	13	7	1.857	8
2	Sheffield Wednesday	4	3	0	1	14	7	2.000	6
3	Nottingham Forest	4	2	2	0	7	4	1.750	6
4	Manchester United	4	2	1	1	10	6	1.667	5
5	Tottenham Hotspur	4	2	1	1	9	8	1.125	5
6	Sheffield United	4	2	1	1	4	4	1.000	5
7	Burnley	4	2	1	1	11	12	0.917	5
8	Everton	4	2	0	2	6	5	1.200	4
9	Arsenal	4	1	2	1	10	10	1.000	4
10	West Ham United	4	1	2	1	7	7	1.000	4
11	Cardiff City	4	1	2	1	4	4	1.000	4
12	**Ipswich Town**	**4**	**1**	**1**	**2**	**11**	**10**	**1.100**	**3**
13	Wolverhampton Wanderers	3	1	1	1	6	6	1.000	3
14	Aston Villa	3	1	1	1	5	5	1.000	3
15	Chelsea	4	1	1	2	7	8	0.875	3
16	Blackpool	4	1	1	2	6	7	0.857	3
17	Leicester City	4	1	1	2	6	8	0.750	3
18	Bolton Wanderers	4	1	1	2	7	10	0.700	3
19	Birmingham City	4	1	1	2	5	9	0.556	3
20	Fulham	4	1	0	3	7	9	0.778	2
21	West Bromwich Albion	4	1	0	3	3	6	0.500	2
22	Blackburn Rovers	4	0	2	2	3	9	0.333	2

Next up was the return fixture with Burnley and few, if any, could have predicted the outcome of a truly incredible game. Not only did Town record their first victory of the season, they did it in magnificent, breathtaking style with an emphatic 6-2 victory that saw all five Ipswich forwards get on the scoresheet for the first time in the club's entire history of League football - if the 1961/62 season had a tuning point, then this was it.

One of the success stories of the game was the performance of full-back John Compton, who was making his start of the campaign as replacement for the injured Ken Malcolm, and completely nullified the threat of Burnley's England international winger John Connelly.

SIX OF
THE BEST
FOR THE CLARETS

TOWN'S FIRST VICTORY IN THE TOP FLIGHT CAME IN SOME STYLE
CRAWFORD CHALLENGES BURNLEY GOALKEEPER BLACKLAW

ROY BAILEY

PLAYER PROFILE

DATE OF BIRTH:	26 May 1932
PLACE OF BIRTH:	Epsom
IPSWICH TOWN (ALL COMPS):	346 Appearances
1961/62 (LEAGUE ONLY):	37 Appearances

Roy Bailey was one of thirteen children and first came to prominence as a goalkeeper at the age of fifteen when he played for Tottenham Hotspur juniors, before eventually signing for Crystal Palace as an amateur, simply because Selhurst Park was located closer to his home.

He made over 100 appearances for the 'Eagles' before being signed by Alf Ramsey in March 1956 and made his first-team debut in a 3-2 defeat against Norwich City at Carrow Road soon afterwards.

Roy quickly became established as Town's first-choice goalkeeper, eventually going on to make almost 350 appearances for the club including 37 of Town's 42 league games in the 1961/62 Division One championship season, when only injury prevented him being an ever-present.

One of the finest goalkeepers in Town's history, Roy's Portman Road career spanned ten seasons, during which he won championship medals in the First, Second and Third Divisions of the Football League.

In 1965 he retired from the game and eventually emigrated to South Africa and lived there until he died in April 1993 aged 60. Roy was inducted into the Ipswich Town Hall of Fame in 2011 and his son Gary carried on the family goalkeeping tradition when he played with distinction for a number of seasons with Manchester United where he made almost 300 first-team league appearances.

ROY
BAILEY

Next up was a visit to The Hawthorns to face a West Bromwich Albion side that included a certain Bobby Robson. The game developed into a dour encounter with little goalmouth action, but midway through the first-half, Crawford seized on a mistake by Wallace in the Albion goal to set up a simple chance for Moran who slotted home from close range.

Then just before the break, Crawford doubled Town's advantage with a brilliant solo goal. Albion came more into the game in the second period and pulled a goal back through Jackson, but soon afterwards Moran grabbed his second to make the points safe for Ipswich.

Three days later, almost 25,000 packed into Portman Road to witness a hard-fought victory over Blackburn Rovers. After Stephenson had given the home side the lead, Phillips doubled their advantage with an absolutely stunning goal, a screaming shot from the edge of the box that fairly rocketed into the net. Shortly before the break, Rovers were awarded a dubious penalty which was duly converted by Douglas. There was no further scoring as Town secured another victory that lifted them to sixth place in the league.

Instead of relegation, thoughts of supporters were now turning to what previously seemed an impossible scenario of a title challenge and a 4-1 victory over Birmingham City in their next game at Portman Road simply fuelled their dreams. Crawford and Phillips were fast gaining a reputation as the most prolific scorers in the league and were again on target with the latter grabbing a brace in a one-sided encounter. Two days later, Ramsey's men gained revenge over Manchester City with a 4-2 victory in the League Cup at Portman Road in only the second-ever game in the competition.

The Ipswich Town rollercoaster was beginning to look unstoppable, but on a hugely disappointing afternoon at Goodison Park it came to a shuddering halt with a 5-2 defeat. The home side dominated proceedings from the start with Irish international right-winger Bill Bingham giving John Compton his most difficult game of the season as his teammate on the opposite flank, Derek Temple, helped himself to a hat-trick. Wilf Hall had deputised in goal for the injured Roy Bailey, but was exonerated from any blame by Alf Ramsey who commented after the game: "All our players, with the notable exception of Wilf Hall, were somewhat off colour. It was a very disappointing display."

Two days later, Ramsey's team were back in action, this time against a star-studded Blackburn Rovers side that included England internationals Ronnie Clayton and Bryan Douglas. Fortunately, the memories of the Goodison Park defeat were quickly eradicated as Town produced a battling performance that saw two goals from Ted Phillips earn a share of the spoils in a 2-2 draw.

THE IPSWICH STRIKER WAS NOW TOP SCORER IN DIVISION ONE WITH NINE GOALS AND THE POINT LIFTED IPSWICH INTO SIXTH PLACE.

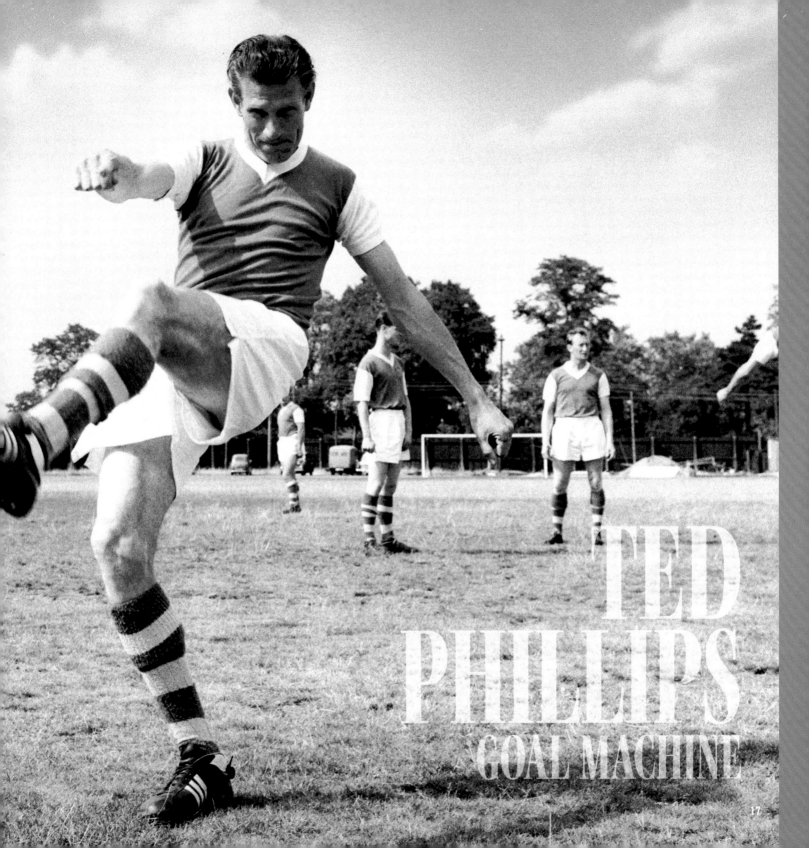

TED
PHILLIPS
GOAL MACHINE

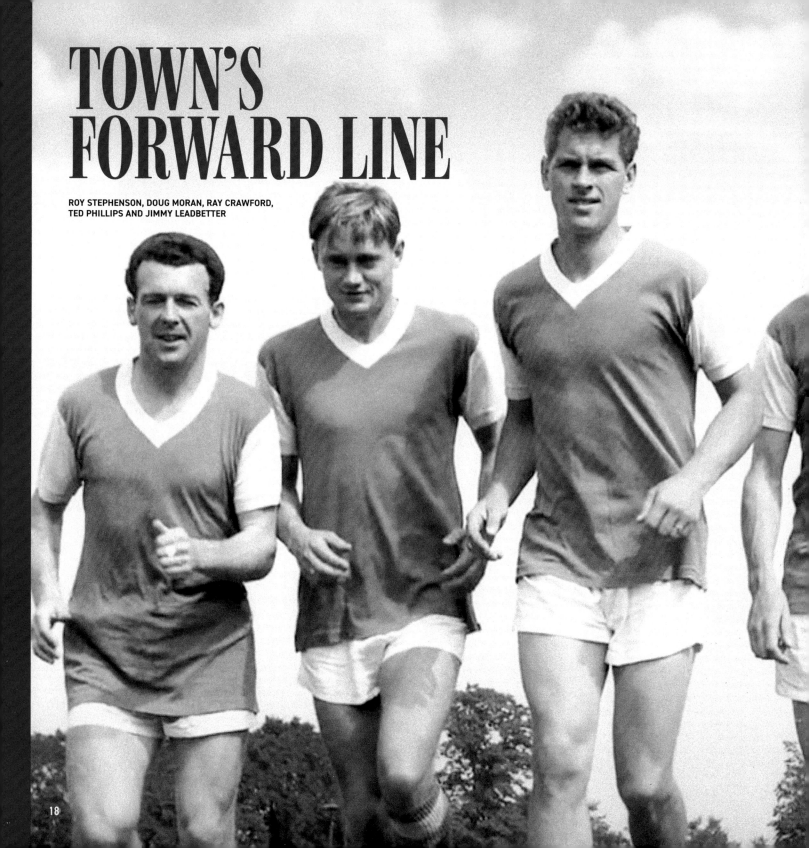

TOWN'S FORWARD LINE

ROY STEPHENSON, DOUG MORAN, RAY CRAWFORD, TED PHILLIPS AND JIMMY LEADBETTER

Back on home soil, Town then came up against a Fulham side that included the highest paid player in English football, Johnny Haynes. In a move designed to stave off strong interest from the top Italian clubs that were circling Craven Cottage, and with the maximum wage having just been abolished, Fulham chairman Tommy Trinder took the bold step of paying the England captain £100 per week, an astronomical sum compared to the previous £20 maximum.

Haynes was an outstanding talent and one of the finest inside forwards in the game as Town would discover to their cost as he produced a brilliant performance to lead his team to a 4-2 victory. Ray Crawford netted both Town goals, but in truth, the visitors fully deserved the points against a below par Ipswich side.

Next up for Town came a tough challenge away to Sheffield Wednesday who had finished as runners-up to Spurs the previous season, yet on the day, Ramsey's men produced an exhilarating performance to record an emphatic 4-1 victory.

The star of the show was undoubtedly Ted Phillips who bagged two goals and was beginning to gain a reputation as possessing the most powerful shot in the English game, a fact emphasised by his second strike which was described by the Evening Star reporter as "the hardest shot I've ever seen!"

DIVISION ONE

	30 SEPTEMBER 1961	P	W	D	L	F	A	GA	P
1	Burnley	11	9	1	1	38	22	1.727	19
2	West Ham United	11	6	3	2	26	18	1.444	15
3	Manchester United	10	6	2	2	20	14	1.429	14
4	Nottingham Forest	11	5	3	3	21	15	1.400	13
5	Manchester City	11	6	1	4	23	22	1.045	13
6	**Ipswich Town**	**11**	**5**	**2**	**4**	**30**	**25**	**1.200**	**12**
7	Tottenham Hotspur	10	5	2	3	15	14	1.071	12
8	Fulham	11	4	3	4	22	22	1.000	11
9	Sheffield Wednesday	10	4	2	4	21	15	1.400	10
10	Cardiff City	11	3	4	4	19	18	1.056	10
11	Everton	11	5	0	6	19	19	1.000	10
12	Bolton Wanderers	11	4	2	5	20	23	0.870	10
13	Blackburn Rovers	11	3	4	4	16	20	0.800	10
14	Sheffield United	10	4	2	4	10	18	0.556	10
15	Wolverhampton Wanderers	10	3	3	4	15	16	0.938	9
16	Blackpool	11	3	3	5	19	22	0.864	9
17	Leicester City	11	4	1	6	18	23	0.783	9
18	Aston Villa	9	3	2	4	17	15	1.133	8
19	West Bromwich Albion	11	3	2	6	15	18	0.833	8
20	Arsenal	10	2	4	4	17	22	0.773	8
21	Chelsea	11	2	3	6	19	24	0.792	7
22	Birmingham City	11	2	3	6	13	28	0.464	7

BILLY BAXTER

PLAYER PROFILE

DATE OF BIRTH:	**23 April 1939**
PLACE OF BIRTH:	**Edinburgh**
IPSWICH TOWN (ALL COMPS):	**459 Appearances · 22 Goals**
1961/62 (LEAGUE ONLY):	**40 Appearances**

A stalwart defender who played in all but two of Town's 1961/62 championship games, Billy Baxter spent eleven years at Portman Road racking up an impressive 459 appearances for the club.

Signed from Broxburn Athletic by Alf Ramsey during the 1960 close-season, Billy made his first-team debut at left-back in a 4-1 victory over Norwich City the following season and quickly became a great favourite with the Portman Road faithful. Occupying either wing-half role with equal good effect, he was almost an ever-present in the Ipswich side throughout the 1960s when only injury kept him out of the side.

Billy left the club in 1971 moving to Hull City. He later played for Watford and Northampton Town followed by a spell in non-league football with Nuneaton Borough before retiring from the game in 1975.

Returning to Scotland, he worked as an engineer with British Telecom. He died in Dunfermline in May 2009 after a long battle with cancer.

Billy was inducted into the Ipswich Town Hall of Fame in 2009.

LARRY CARBERRY

PLAYER PROFILE

DATE OF BIRTH:	**18 January 1936**
PLACE OF BIRTH:	**Liverpool**
IPSWICH TOWN (ALL COMPS):	**283 Appearances**
1961/62 (LEAGUE ONLY):	**42 Appearances**

After leaving school, Liverpool-born Larry Carberry initially played for Everton as an amateur before joining Ipswich Town in May 1956.

Larry made his first-team debut in a 4-0 victory over Queens Park Rangers at Portman Road a few months later and quickly earned a reputation as a dependable tough-tackling defender. He played in every game in the 1961/62 championship-winning season having also picked up Division Three (South) and Division Two championship medals in 1956/57 and 1960/61 respectively.

For the best part of nine seasons, Larry was a regular fixture in Town's number two shirt before finally severing his ties with the club to join Barrow in 1965. After retiring from the professional

game he returned to Merseyside where he continued to play in local non-league football.

Larry was inducted into the Ipswich Town Hall of Fame in 2010 and died in June 2015 aged 79.

As September drew to a close, Town were sitting in sixth place in Division One and, after coming back from three goals down to earn a 3-3 draw against Swansea Town in the League Cup, 28,059 fans packed into Portman Road for the next league fixture against West Ham United.

The Hammer's side included Bobby Moore and Geoff Hurst, two men who would become true legends of the English game when they helped England lift the World Cup in 1966, Whilst the fans were treated to six goals, the game itself wasn't much of a spectacle with all the real action taking place in the final third of the game as Ray Crawford and Ted Phillips bagged two goals apiece to earn the home side a well-deserved 4-2 victory. The game also saw Phillips set a new Ipswich Town goalscoring record of 146 goals in just 202 games.

The Town strikers were certainly beginning to catch the headlines and were described by the East Anglian Daily Times as 'the two most deadly marksmen in the modern English game'. However, when Town travelled up to Sheffield to play United at Bramall Lane the following Saturday, it seemed as though Crawford and Phillips had left their shooting boots behind as both were guilty of missing a number of presentable chances. It was a game that Ipswich should have won comfortably, but poor finishing cost them dearly as they slumped to a disappointing 2-1 defeat.

Next up came arguably the most awaited fixture of the season, the visit to Portman Road of Alf Ramsey's former club Tottenham Hotspur. While Burnley were early front runners in Division One, Spurs were still regarded as the finest team in the land, having just become the first side in the twentieth century to win the coveted league and cup double. Town's all-time record attendance was broken and the 28,778 supporters inside Portman Road were certainly not disappointed as both teams served up some brilliant football with Town coming from behind to take the points in a dramatic 3-2 triumph. Whilst Ray Crawford (2) and Ted Phillips grabbed the goals, Town had to thank goalkeeper Roy Bailey for preserving their lead with a string of brilliant saves near the end as Spurs surged forward looking for an equaliser."

Alf Ramsey was full of praise for both teams after the game: "It was a truly great match and a tremendous second half. Although we won and are naturally more than pleased, tribute must be paid to Tottenham, a very fine side indeed.

His Spurs counterpart and former While Hart Lane colleague Bill Nicholson said simply: "If we'd had Ipswich's two goalscoring forwards, we would have paralysed them!"

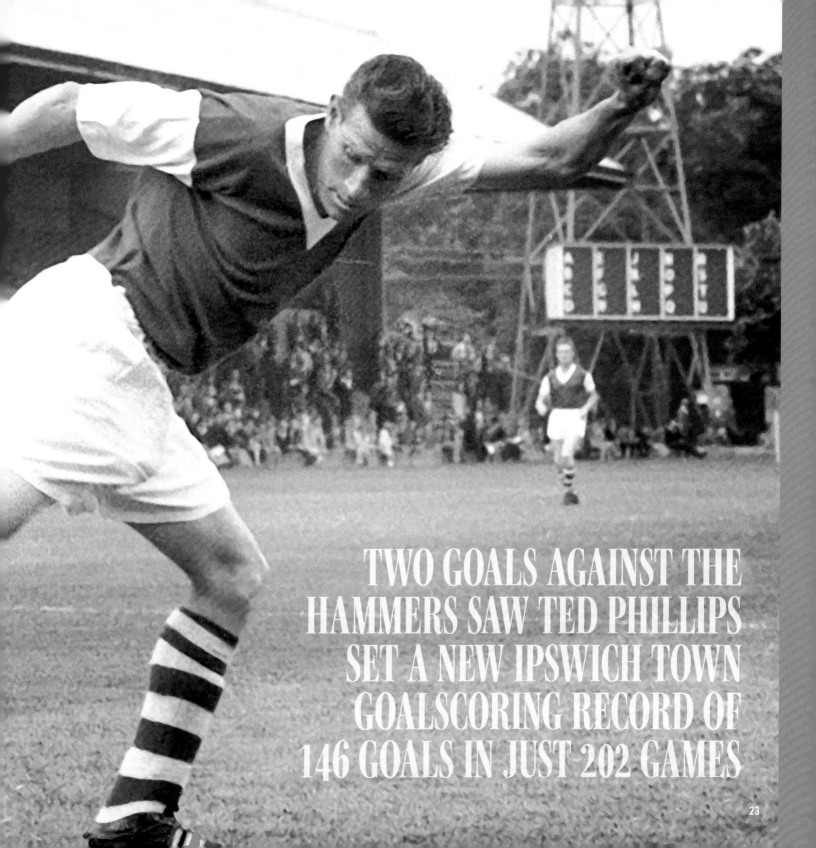

TWO GOALS AGAINST THE HAMMERS SAW TED PHILLIPS SET A NEW IPSWICH TOWN GOALSCORING RECORD OF 146 GOALS IN JUST 202 GAMES

LARRY CARBERRY LEAP-FROGS JOHN COMPTON
DURING A TRAINING SESSION

ROY STEPHENSON

After a narrow 3-2 win over Swansea Town in a League Cup second round replay, Town made yet another long trip up to Lancashire, this time to face Blackpool at Bloomfield Road. The game turned out to be a disappointing affair and after Ted Phillips gave them an early lead they failed to press home their advantage and paid the price with just eight minutes remaining when Parry netted an equaliser for the home side.

The East Anglian Daily times carried the headline: "Half-hearted performance at Blackpool!" Nevertheless, as October drew to a close, Town were sitting fourth in the table, four points behind leaders Burnley who had lost 4-2 at Tottenham.

DIVISION ONE

	31 OCTOBER 1961	P	W	D	L	F	A	GA	P
1	Burnley	14	10	1	3	43	29	1.483	21
2	Tottenham Hotspur	14	8	2	4	25	20	1.250	18
3	Everton	15	8	1	6	30	20	1.500	17
4	**Ipswich Town**	**15**	**7**	**3**	**5**	**39**	**32**	**1.219**	**17**
5	Fulham	15	6	5	4	30	26	1.154	17
6	West Ham United	15	7	3	5	32	28	1.143	17
7	Sheffield Wednesday	14	7	2	5	30	21	1.429	16
8	Manchester City	15	7	1	7	28	30	0.933	15
9	Nottingham Forest	15	5	5	5	26	29	0.897	15
10	Manchester United	14	6	3	5	22	25	0.880	15
11	Arsenal	14	4	6	4	26	24	1.083	14
12	Cardiff City	15	4	6	5	25	24	1.042	14
13	Bolton Wanderers	15	6	2	7	26	27	0.963	14
14	Blackpool	15	5	4	6	24	27	0.889	14
15	Wolverhampton Wanderers	15	5	3	7	25	25	1.000	13
16	Aston Villa	14	5	3	6	22	22	1.000	13
17	Leicester City	15	6	1	8	26	29	0.897	13
18	Blackburn Rovers	14	4	5	5	18	22	0.818	13
19	Birmingham City	15	5	3	7	24	37	0.649	13
20	Sheffield United	14	5	3	6	15	26	0.577	13
21	West Bromwich Albion	15	3	6	6	23	26	0.885	12
22	Chelsea	15	2	4	9	26	36	0.722	8

The following week Ramsey's men again produced another somewhat lacklustre performance, this time against Nottingham Forest at Portman Road. Phillips again gave them a first-half lead but thereafter they were very much second best to a Forest side who really should have taken something from the game. Twice the visitors had goals disallowed for offside then, with eight minutes to go, they were awarded a penalty only for Palmer to see his weak effort palmed away to safety by Bailey.

TED PHILLIPS

PLAYER PROFILE

DATE OF BIRTH:	**21 August 1933**
PLACE OF BIRTH:	**Snape, Suffolk**
IPSWICH TOWN (ALL COMPS):	**293 Appearances · 179 goals**
1961/62 (LEAGUE ONLY):	**40 Appearances · 28 goals**

Ironically, Ted Phillips was the only local player in the 1961/62 team having joined the club from Leiston in December 1953.

Ted was involved in both of Town's Division Three (South) triumphs as well as the subsequent Division Two and Division One successes. A prolific goalscorer throughout his time at Portman Road, he netted no fewer than 46 goals during the 1956/57 campaign, a club record that still stands to this day.

The trademark of Ted's game was his powerful shooting and at his peak he was widely regarded as the hardest striker of a ball in the English game. Ted was also the club's regular penalty-taker netting twenty-five out of twenty-eight attempts during his Ipswich career. Throughout the late 1950s and 1960s, he and strike-partner Ray Crawford scored goals for fun including no fewer than 61 of Town's 93 goals in the 1961/62 Division One championship-winning season.

Ted's lengthy and hugely successful Town career finally came to an end in March 1964 when he joined Leyton Orient. Spells with Luton Town and Colchester United followed before he joined Maltese side Floriana as player manager.

Ted remains one of the greatest goalscorers in the history of Ipswich Town and was inducted into the club's Hall of Fame in 2007. He died in January 2018, aged 84

TED
PHILLIPS

Next up was a visit to Wolverhampton Wanderers, an outstanding side of the period who had lifted the league title twice in the late 50s as well as the FA Cup in 1960. Unfortunately, Town were hampered almost from the start when, with only six minutes on the clock, Roy Stephenson was forced off with a thigh strain and was unable to play any further part in the game.

Given that this was an era prior to substitutes being allowed, Ramsey's men had no alternative, but to soldier on with ten men and their brave rearguard action almost earned an unlikely point until Wolves finally broke the deadlock on 69 minutes when Hinton's cross was headed home by Wharton. Town threw everyone forward looking for an equaliser, but in the dying minutes the home side secured victory when Hinton broke clear and netted from close range.

Roy Stephenson was still missing for Town's next game, the much awaited visit of Manchester United who were still in the process of rebuilding after the tragedy of Munich three years earlier. Nevertheless, United manager Matt Busby was still able to call on a number of international players including Bobby Charlton, Bill Foulkes and Warren Bradley and the likes of Nobby Stiles, Johnny Giles, Tony Dunne and Shay Brennan all of whom would go on to represent their country.

For Town, Dermot Curtis was brought in for his first game of the season as a replacement for the injured Stephenson, while up in the stands England manager Walter Winterbottom took his seat to no doubt run the rule over Ray Crawford who was topping the goalscoring charts in Division One.

Whilst Crawford enjoyed an excellent game and was one of Town's scorers in a 4-1 victory, the England boss could not have failed to have been impressed by the powerhouse shooting of Ted Phillips who grabbed a brace, with a rare goal from John Elsworthy completing the route.

A few days later, Town progressed to the next round of the League Cup with an impressive 3-2 victory over Aston Villa at Villa Park. Ray Crawford missed the tie having been selected to play for England against Northern Ireland the following day. It was a momentous occasion for the Town striker who became the first Ipswich Town player ever to be selected to play for England at full international level.

Crawford was back leading the line in Town's next game, a comfortable 3-0 victory over Cardiff City at Ninian Park. Ted Phillips again bagged a couple of goals, his first a tremendous thunderbolt effort from outside the box that had the striker celebrating wildly.

The victory moved Alf Ramsey's men into second place in Division One, just three points behind the league leaders Burnley.

DIVISION ONE

30 NOVEMBER 1961		P	W	D	L	F	A	GA	P
1	Burnley	18	12	2	4	55	36	1.528	26
2	**Ipswich Town**	**19**	**10**	**3**	**6**	**47**	**35**	**1.343**	**23**
3	Everton	19	10	2	7	36	24	1.500	22
4	West Ham United	19	9	4	6	43	39	1.103	22
5	Sheffield Wednesday	19	9	3	7	37	26	1.423	21
6	Tottenham Hotspur	18	9	3	6	30	27	1.111	21
7	Leicester City	19	9	2	8	36	32	1.125	20
8	Arsenal	19	7	6	6	33	33	1.000	20
9	Fulham	19	7	5	7	34	32	1.063	19
10	Bolton Wanderers	19	8	3	8	30	29	1.034	19
11	Aston Villa	18	7	4	7	28	28	1.000	18
12	Cardiff City	19	6	6	7	28	31	0.903	18
13	Blackpool	19	6	6	7	28	32	0.875	18
14	West Bromwich Albion	19	5	7	7	34	34	1.000	17
15	Nottingham Forest	19	6	5	8	30	35	0.857	17
16	Sheffield United	18	7	3	8	22	33	0.667	17
17	Wolverhampton Wanderers	19	6	4	9	32	34	0.941	16
18	Manchester City	19	7	2	10	35	42	0.833	16
19	Manchester United	18	6	4	8	27	38	0.711	16
20	Birmingham City	19	6	4	9	30	43	0.698	16
21	Chelsea	19	5	5	9	36	39	0.923	15
22	Blackburn Rovers	18	5	5	8	20	29	0.690	15

Town began December with an emphatic 5-2 victory over Chelsea who arrived at Portman Road under the leadership of new manager Tommy Docherty. While 'The Pensioners' boasted a number of future internationals, including Peter Bonetti and Bobby Tambling, they were no match for a rampant Ipswich team that saw Ray Crawford again grab the headlines with another hat-trick.

The result consolidated Town's second place in the table behind Burnley, but a week later they slipped behind in the race when they were soundly beaten 3-0 by Aston Villa at Villa Park. Northern Ireland international winger Peter McParland was their tormentor in chief, bagging a couple of goals and generally giving the Town defence a torrid afternoon with his surging runs down the left flank.

REG PICKETT

DATE OF BIRTH:	**6 January 1927**
PLACE OF BIRTH:	**India**
IPSWICH TOWN (ALL COMPS):	**146 Appearances · 3 Goals**
1961/62 (LEAGUE ONLY):	**3 Appearances**

Reg Pickett was the only member of the 1961/62 squad to have previously won a Division One championship medal, which he won with Portsmouth in their triumphant 1949/50 season.

Signed from Pompey at the end of the 1956/57 season, Reg was a truly versatile player who although predominantly a wing-half, could play in virtually any position on the field.

Soon after signing, Alf Ramsey made him captain, a position he held until 1960 when he handed the role to Andy Nelson. Reg only managed three league appearances during the 1961/62 Division One campaign, deputising for first Bill Baxter and then John Elsworthy.

By then he was very much a fringe player in the squad and in 1963 his career at Portman Road came to an end when he moved into non-league football to join Stevenage Town.

He eventually returned to Portsmouth where he lived in retirement until his death in November 2012, aged 85.

ALED OWEN

DATE OF BIRTH:	**7 January 1934**
PLACE OF BIRTH:	**Anglesey**
IPSWICH TOWN (ALL COMPS):	**34 Appearances · 3 Goals**
1961/62 (LEAGUE ONLY):	**1 Appearance**

Aled Owen made only one league appearance during the 1961/62 Division One championship-winning season when he deputised for the injured Jimmy Leadbetter in the Boxing Day victory over Leicester City.

Signed from Spurs in 1958, Aled spent five years with Town, but for the duration his time at Portman Road he was very much a fringe player in Alf Ramsey's squad and in 1963 he returned to Wales to join Wrexham.

TEAM PHOTOGRAPH BEFORE THE LEAGUE DIVISION TWO GAME AGAINST BRIGHTON & HOVE ALBION AT THE GOLDSTONE GROUND, 7 SEPTEMBER 1960.

BACK ROW L TO R: LAWRENCE CARBERRY, REGINALD PICKETT, JOHN ELSWORTHY, WILFRED HALL, ANDREW NELSON AND KENNETH MALCOLM.

FRONT ROW: ALED OWEN, WILLIAMS REES, RAY CRAWFORD, TED PHILLIPS AND JAMES LEADBETTER.

31

Interest in the League Cup ended a few days later with another heavy defeat, this time against Blackburn Rovers at Ewood Park, who were good value for their 4-1 victory. The following Saturday saw Bolton Wanderers arrive for their first-ever visit to Portman Road and just as they had in the opening game of the season, the Lancashire side proved to be a tough nut to crack.

For long periods, Town struggled to come to terms with Wanderer's 'rough-house' tactics and after the visitors took a first-half lead through Doug Holden, the points appeared to be heading north until a dramatic finale that had the home fans celebrating wildly.

With only seven minutes remaining, Town drew level in controversial fashion when Crawford bundled the ball home after Wanderers 'keeper Hopkinson had dropped Stephenson's corner. The visitors besieged the referee claiming the ball had not crossed the line, but the goal stood and worse was to follow for the Lancashire side when Town grabbed the victory with only two minutes remaining.

With the home side laying siege on Wanderers goal, the ball broke to Moran whose powerful shot was only blocked by Hopkinson for Crawford to move in and hammer the ball home. The victory was even sweeter given the visitor's tactics with the East Anglian Daily Times summing up the game perfectly with the headline: 'Good Triumphs Over Evil'!

Two days before Christmas, when Town travelled up to Manchester to face a City side who were languishing in the lower reaches of Division One, two points looked to be a formality, However, a below-par performance by Ramsey's men saw the home side record an emphatic 3-0 victory with 17-year-old Neil Young crowning an outstanding display with a superb goal.

A few days later, on Boxing Day, they managed to get back to winning ways with a hard-fought 1-0 victory over Leicester City at Portman Road. Welshman Aled Owen made his only league appearance of the season replacing Jimmy Leadbetter who had picked up knee injury at Maine Road, the first time the Ipswich winger had been missing from the Town line-up in 156 games.

Ironically, it was Owen who set up the only goal of the game on 67 minutes, crossing for Ray Crawford to hook the ball past City 'keeper Gordon Banks. After that, Town were forced into some desperate defending and needed a last-minute goal-line clearance by Carberry to preserve their lead.

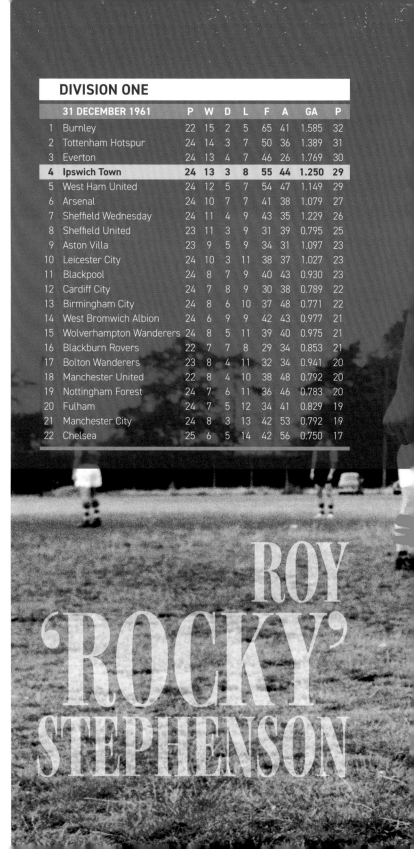

DIVISION ONE

31 DECEMBER 1961	P	W	D	L	F	A	GA	P
1 Burnley	22	15	2	5	65	41	1.585	32
2 Tottenham Hotspur	24	14	3	7	50	36	1.389	31
3 Everton	24	13	4	7	46	26	1.769	30
4 Ipswich Town	24	13	3	8	55	44	1.250	29
5 West Ham United	24	12	5	7	54	47	1.149	29
6 Arsenal	24	10	7	7	41	38	1.079	27
7 Sheffield Wednesday	24	11	4	9	43	35	1.229	26
8 Sheffield United	23	11	3	9	31	39	0.795	25
9 Aston Villa	23	9	5	9	34	31	1.097	23
10 Leicester City	24	10	3	11	38	37	1.027	23
11 Blackpool	24	8	7	9	40	43	0.930	23
12 Cardiff City	24	7	8	9	30	38	0.789	22
13 Birmingham City	24	8	6	10	37	48	0.771	22
14 West Bromwich Albion	24	6	9	9	42	43	0.977	21
15 Wolverhampton Wanderers	24	8	5	11	39	40	0.975	21
16 Blackburn Rovers	22	7	7	8	29	34	0.853	21
17 Bolton Wanderers	23	8	4	11	32	34	0.941	20
18 Manchester United	22	8	4	10	38	48	0.792	20
19 Nottingham Forest	24	7	6	11	36	46	0.783	20
20 Fulham	24	7	5	12	34	41	0.829	19
21 Manchester City	24	8	3	13	42	53	0.792	19
22 Chelsea	25	6	5	14	42	56	0.750	17

ROY 'ROCKY' STEPHENSON

January saw Town turn their attention to FA Cup glory and a home tie with Second Division Luton Town. A goal by Ted Phillips in the first minute seemed to have them on their way but 'The Hatters' proved to be resilient opponents and deservedly equalised in the second half to secure a 1-1.

The replay at Kenilworth Road a few days later followed pretty much the same pattern with John Elsworthy opening the scoring with a twenty-yard strike after sixteen minutes, only for Pacey to grab a late equaliser for the home side. With thirty minutes extra time producing no further goals, the tie was destined for a second replay at Arsenal's Highbury ground.

Before that however, Town were back in league action, this time producing one of their best performances of the season to record an emphatic 3-0 victory over West Bromwich Albion at Portman Road.

Stephenson in particular was in great form, opening the scoring in the first half with a great finish from a narrow angle and then setting up the second goal for Moran just after the break. Leadbetter completed the scoring in the final minute to secure a victory that saw Ramsey's men move into third place in the table.

Two days later, Ramsey's men finally saw off the challenge of Luton Town with a 5-1 victory at Highbury to set up a mouth-watering fourth round tie against arch-rivals Norwich City. Wilf Hall had stood in for Roy Bailey who was suffering with tonsillitis and continued in goal for the following game against Birmingham City at St. Andrews. Sadly, he was unable to stop the home side recording an unlikely 3-1 victory, a result that saw Town slip down to fourth place in Division One, four points behind leaders Burnley.

Next up, it was back to FA Cup action and the much-awaited fourth round tie against Norwich City at Carrow Road. A crowd of almost 40,000 packed into the Second Division club's ground to witness a nail-biting encounter that saw the home side take the lead just after the break when Allcock beat Nelson in the air to head home.

Five minutes later however, Leadbetter levelled the scores when he beat Thurlow before rounding Kennon to slot the ball home. With no further scoring, the tie moved to Portman Road a few days later and again it developed into a hard-fought encounter.

Yet again it was Allcock who proved to be Town's tormentor in chief giving City a first-half lead and then netting the winner in the dying minutes after Crawford had levelled the tie. It was a heart-breaking night for Town fans in what was undoubtedly their biggest disappointment of the season.

WILF HALL

PLAYER PROFILE

DATE OF BIRTH:	**14 October 1934**
PLACE OF BIRTH:	**St. Helens**
IPSWICH TOWN (ALL COMPS):	**19 Appearances**
1961/62 (LEAGUE ONLY):	**5 Appearances**

St. Helens-born Wilf Hall signed from Stoke City in June 1960, and after making his Ipswich Town debut in a 4-1 victory over Derby County, the future certainly looked bright for the young 'keeper.

However, the outstanding form of Roy Bailey meant that Wilf rarely had an opportunity to stake his claim for regular first-team football. He made just five appearances during the 1961/62 Division One championship-winning season when he deputised for Bailey who was out of the side due to injury.

This was pretty much the picture throughout Wilf's three years at Portman Road and in 1963, after making just 19 appearances for the Club, he decided to sever his ties with Ipswich Town and move into non-league football with Macclesfield Town.

Wilf died in August 2007 at the age of 72.

JOHN ELSWORTHY

PLAYER PROFILE

DATE OF BIRTH:	**26 July 1931**
PLACE OF BIRTH:	**Nant-y-derry**
IPSWICH TOWN (ALL COMPS):	**433 Appearances · 52 Goals**
1961/62 (LEAGUE ONLY):	**41 Appearances · 2 Goals**

A great servant to Ipswich Town, wing-half John Elsworthy was a cultured footballer who became a fixture in the side for the best part of his sixteen years at the club.

Spotted playing for Newport County's youth team, John signed for Town in May 1949 and made his first-team debut in a 4-0 defeat against Notts County at Portman Road a few months later.

Despite standing 6' 3", John could never be described as a physical player and was known throughout the game as very much a 'gentle giant' who preferred to let his football do the talking. During his Portman Road career, John picked up a record haul of two Division Three (South) championship medals, one Division Two championship medal and, of course, a Division One championship medal in 1961/62.

At his peak, he was widely regarded as one of the finest wing-halves in the game and could count himself unlucky not to have been capped by Wales at senior level.

Ipswich Town were John's only professional club and after hanging up his boots he remained in the area where he ran a post office until his retirement.

Inducted into the Ipswich Town Hall of Fame in 2008, John died in May 2009 aged 77.

DIVISION ONE

31 JANUARY 1962		P	W	D	L	F	A	GA	P
1	Burnley	24	16	3	5	72	45	1.600	35
2	Tottenham Hotspur	26	14	5	7	53	39	1.359	33
3	Everton	26	14	4	8	50	31	1.613	32
4	**Ipswich Town**	**26**	**14**	**3**	**9**	**59**	**47**	**1.255**	**31**
5	West Ham United	26	13	5	8	56	50	1.120	31
6	Sheffield Wednesday	26	13	4	9	48	36	1.333	30
7	Sheffield United	25	12	4	9	34	40	0.850	28
8	Blackpool	26	10	7	9	48	45	1.067	27
9	Arsenal	26	10	7	9	44	43	1.023	27
10	Birmingham City	26	10	6	10	42	50	0.840	26
11	Blackburn Rovers	24	9	7	8	33	35	0.943	25
12	Aston Villa	26	9	6	11	34	35	0.971	24
13	Cardiff City	26	7	10	9	32	40	0.800	24
14	Leicester City	26	10	3	13	41	42	0.976	23
15	Bolton Wanderers	25	9	5	11	35	36	0.972	23
16	Manchester United	25	9	5	11	42	51	0.824	23
17	West Bromwich Albion	26	6	10	10	43	47	0.915	22
18	Nottingham Forest	26	8	6	12	40	48	0.833	22
19	Wolverhampton Wanderers	26	8	5	13	41	49	0.837	21
20	Manchester City	26	9	3	14	48	61	0.787	21
21	Fulham	26	7	5	14	37	47	0.787	19
22	Chelsea	27	7	5	15	47	62	0.758	19

Any doubts about how Ramsey's men would react to this shattering defeat were soon dispelled in their next game when they produced some of their best football of the season to record a 4-2 victory over Everton at Portman Road.

Prior to the game, it had been strongly rumoured that Ramsey was about to drop Ted Phillips who had been suffering a poor run of form, but his decision to keep the Town striker in the side was vindicated after only six minutes when he gave the home side an early lead.

Further goals from Moran, Elsworthy and Crawford completed a fine victory that began a run of sixteen games during which Town only lost once more before the end of the campaign.

Earlier in the season, a Johnny Haynes inspired Fulham side had recorded a comprehensive victory at Portman Road, but in the return fixture at Craven Cottage, Town exacted revenge with a narrow 2-1 victory. Future England international Alan Mullery gave the home side the lead, but goals from Stephenson and Crawford secured the points but only after an outstanding performance from 'keeper Roy Bailey had kept the home side at bay.

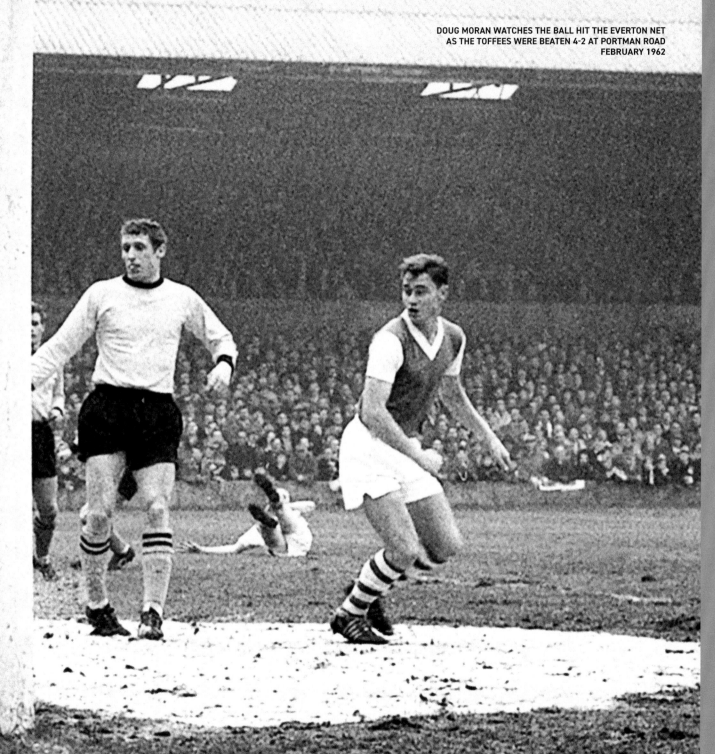

DOUG MORAN WATCHES THE BALL HIT THE EVERTON NET
AS THE TOFFEES WERE BEATEN 4-2 AT PORTMAN ROAD
FEBRUARY 1962

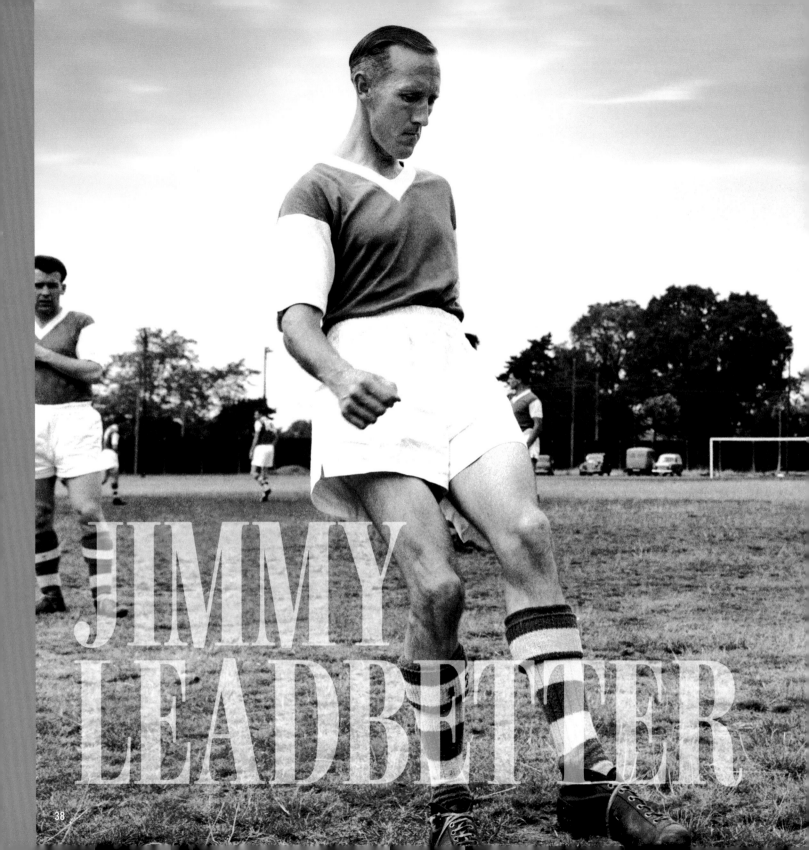

JIMMY
LEADBETTER

JIMMY LEADBETTER

DATE OF BIRTH:	**28 July 1928**
PLACE OF BIRTH:	**Edinburgh**
IPSWICH TOWN (ALL COMPS):	**373 Appearances · 49 goals**
1961/62 (LEAGUE ONLY):	**41 Appearances · 8 goals**

Jimmy Leadbetter was about as far removed from the modern archetypal professional footballer as you could imagine.

Slightly built with spindly legs that earned him the nickname 'sticks' and looking much older than his 34 years, he was, nevertheless, a key player in the 1961/62 Division One championship-winning team and one who was held in high regard by Manager Alf Ramsey.

A vastly experienced player, Jimmy began his career south of the border with Chelsea after signing from Armadale Thistle in 1949. After three seasons at Stamford Bridge, he joined Brighton and Hove Albion before being snapped up by Town boss Scott Duncan in June 1955. It was to be Duncan's last significant act as manager and within a few weeks he was replaced by Alf Ramsey, a man who was about to revolutionise Jimmy's career.

Previously used as a traditional inside-forward, Town's new boss persuaded Jimmy to operate as a deep-lying winger, a tactic unheard of in the game at that time, but one which would work to devastating affect in the years ahead. Although not particularly fast, Jimmy's ability to win the ball, his accuracy of passing and ability to deliver pin-point crosses for the likes of Ray Crawford and Ted Phillips, more than compensated his lack of pace.

During his ten-year Portman Road career, he was one of only three players to win Division Three (South), Division Two and Division One championship medals. After leaving Town in 1965, Jimmy played with Sudbury Town until he was forty three years old and also enjoyed a spell managing the non-league side. He then returned to Edinburgh where he lived in quiet retirement until his death in July 2006. Two years later he was inducted into the Ipswich Town Hall of Fame.

ROY BAILEY, JOHN ELSWORTHY, LARRY CARBERRY, TED PHILLIPS AND JIMMY LEADBETTER

40

Two weeks later, Town were back in London again, this time to face a West Ham United side who were enjoying a fine season and were sitting in fifth place in Division One. As expected, this game developed into a close contest with Ipswich twice coming from behind to grab a point in a 2-2 draw, with goals from Leadbetter and a late penalty converted in typical fashion by Phillips.

DIVISION ONE

	28 FEBRUARY 1962	P	W	D	L	F	A	GA	P
1	Burnley	28	18	4	6	84	51	1.647	40
2	Tottenham Hotspur	30	15	7	8	60	46	1.304	37
3	**Ipswich Town**	**29**	**16**	**4**	**9**	**67**	**52**	**1.288**	**36**
4	West Ham United	30	14	7	9	62	56	1.107	35
5	Sheffield United	29	15	5	9	41	43	0.953	35
6	Everton	29	14	5	10	55	39	1.410	33
7	Aston Villa	30	12	7	11	39	36	1.083	31
8	Sheffield Wednesday	29	13	4	12	50	41	1.220	30
9	Blackburn Rovers	28	11	8	9	38	37	1.027	30
10	Manchester United	29	12	6	11	53	54	0.981	30
11	Blackpool	30	11	7	12	53	52	1.019	29
12	Arsenal	29	11	7	11	45	45	1.000	29
13	Leicester City	30	12	4	14	50	49	1.020	28
14	Wolverhampton Wanderers	30	11	6	13	51	55	0.927	28
15	Birmingham City	30	11	6	13	47	62	0.758	28
16	West Bromwich Albion	30	8	10	12	52	56	0.929	26
17	Bolton Wanderers	29	10	6	13	42	48	0.875	26
18	Nottingham Forest	30	10	6	14	49	58	0.845	26
19	Manchester City	30	11	4	15	53	64	0.828	26
20	Cardiff City	30	7	11	12	35	48	0.729	25
21	Chelsea	31	9	5	17	49	66	0.742	23
22	Fulham	30	7	5	18	40	57	0.702	19

March began with two home games, ironically, against both Sheffield sides that produced two vital victories to sustain Town's challenge for top spot. First, United were swept aside as goals from Moran, Leadbetter and a brace from Crawford secured an emphatic 4-0 win, and then Wednesday were beaten, although this game was a much closer affair.

After an early goal from the visitors, Town struggled to get back into the game and had to wait until the half-hour mark for Crawford to level the scores. The game appeared to be heading for a draw when, with only four minutes remaining, Stephenson finally broke Wednesday's resolve, racing onto Crawford's through ball to fire home the winner. The one downside to the victory was the sight of Billy Baxter being stretchered from the pitch with a suspected broken leg.

Five days later came arguably Town's toughest test of the season when they came up against Tottenham Hotspur at White Hart Lane who were no doubt in search of revenge following their 3-2 defeat at Portman Road earlier in the campaign.

Ramsey's men were given a huge boost before the game with the news that Billy Baxter had only suffered severe bruising against Sheffield Wednesday and was available for selection, allowing the Ipswich boss to name a full-strength team. At Portman Road the two sides had produced a magnificent display of fast, attacking football and a huge crowd of over 51,000 packed the North London ground no doubt hoping for another classic encounter.

A large number of Ipswich fans had made the journey in special chartered trains and after only eight minutes they were celebrating wildly when Crawford beat Norman and raced through to beat Brown all ends up. Their joy was short-lived however when only a few minutes later, Greaves levelled the scores with a typical close-range effort after being sent clear by Blanchflower.

The game was now on a knife-edge with Town being forced into some desperate defending, but the game suddenly switched to the opposite end with Stephenson sending a terrific effort against the crossbar. A few minutes later they were back again when a mistake by Norman allowed Stephenson to break clear and cross for Phillips to head home at the far post.

The furious pace continued after the break with both sides missing decent opportunities to score but with the game entering the final stages Crawford sent Phillips through to score with a measured shot from a narrow angle to secure a vital victory. After the game a delighted Alf Ramsey said:

"It was a magnificent performance. We always looked like getting the result and everyone played very well. It was the best victory in the history of the club!"

After such an impressive performance, it was perhaps inevitable the Town's next game, the visit of Blackpool at Portman Road, would be something of an anti-climax. Nevertheless, despite failing to produce anything like the quality of football that had swept Spurs aside, the points appeared to be in the bag after a Doug Moran goal had given them an early lead, only for Charnley to grab a last-minute equaliser for the visitors. To add to their misery, Ted Phillips sustained a broken thumb after falling awkwardly which would keep him out of the next game away to Nottingham Forest.

Dermot Curtis was drafted into the side as Phillips' replacement and the Irish international had a hand in the opening goal scored by Moran midway through the first half. The lead lasted until just before the break when Rowland crossed for Julians to beat Bailey with an assured finish.

Once again Town were forced to defend in depth in the second period with Bailey in particular enjoying an outstanding game to keep the home side at bay. It was a point that Ramsey's men barely deserved after a below-par performance, particularly in the second period, prompting the headline in the East Anglian Daily Times: 'Bailey Earns Ipswich Point at Nottingham'.

A few days later Ramsey and his team were back in the Midlands this time to face Leicester City at Filbert Street for the rearranged fixture after the original game in December had been postponed due to adverse weather. Ted Phillips was still missing from the Ipswich line-up for a game that turned out to be a fast, thrilling encounter with Town very much back to their best form.

They took the lead after only eight minutes when Moran's pin-point cross picked out Crawford racing into the box to send a bullet-header past future England goalkeeper Gordon Banks.

The game then developed into an end-to-end contest with both sides going close before Stephenson doubled Town's advantage just after the break, shooting through a crowd of players after the ball had dropped kindly for him on the edge of the box. Thereafter, the visitors were very much in control, eventually cruising to a comfortable 2-0 victory.

Town were given a huge boost the following Saturday when Ted Phillips was declared fit for the visit of Wolverhampton Wanderers, and the Ipswich striker wasted no time in making his mark in a game that would literally go down in Ipswich Town history. With twenty minutes played they opened the scoring when Phillips netted from the spot after Slater had wrestled Crawford to the ground, but the lead was short-lived as the visitors quickly levelled when Flowers volleyed home from the edge of the box.

The game continued at breathtaking pace with Crawford putting Town ahead only for Wolves to bounce back through new signing Peter McParland. In the second half, the visitors were much the better side, but with only two minutes remaining Moran sealed the victory, slotting the ball home at the far post as Crawford's shot appeared to be going wide. Arguably, Wanderers had been the better side, but Town fans weren't bothered as the victory had taken their team to the top spot for the very first time in their history.

DERMOT CURTIS

PLAYER PROFILE

DATE OF BIRTH:	**26 August 1932**
PLACE OF BIRTH:	**Dublin**
IPSWICH TOWN (ALL COMPS):	**42 Appearances · 17 Goals**
1961/62 (LEAGUE ONLY):	**4 Appearances**

Dublin-born centre-forward Dermot Curtis was already a full international when he was signed from Bristol City by Alf Ramsey in August 1958.

An outstanding forward with an eye for goal, Dermot spent five seasons at Portman Road eventually going on to win 17 caps for his country, but his first-team opportunities for Town were somewhat limited following the emergence of the Ray Crawford/Ted Phillips strike partnership.

His best season was undoubtedly 1959/60 when he netted ten goals including an outstanding display in the 6-1 demolition of Sunderland when he and Ted Phillips became the first-ever Ipswich Town players to net hat-tricks in the same match.

Dermot played only four games in the 1961/62 season and finally left the club in May 1963 when he signed for Exeter City.

He then had a spell with Torquay United before returning to Exeter where he lived in retirement until his death in November 2008, aged 76.

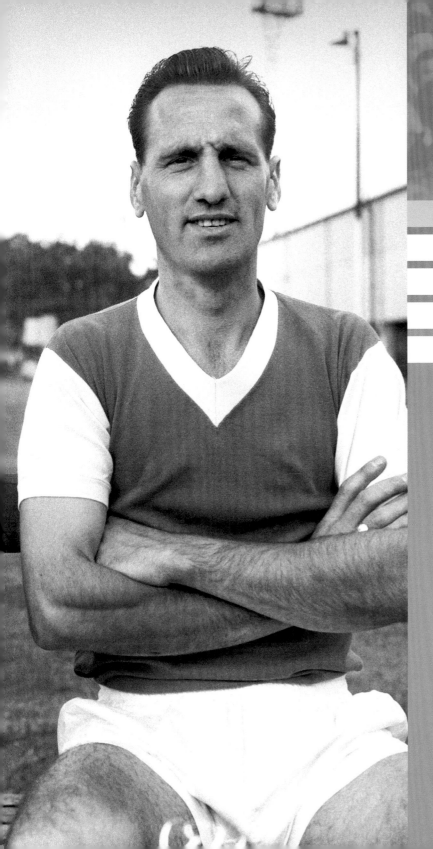

ANDY NELSON

PLAYER PROFILE

DATE OF BIRTH:	**5 July 1935**
PLACE OF BIRTH:	**Custom House, London**
IPSWICH TOWN (ALL COMPS):	**214 Appearances**
1961/62 (LEAGUE ONLY):	**42 Appearances**

A rugged central-defender and captain of the 1961/62 Division One championship-winning team, Andy Nelson gave Ipswich Town sterling service during his five years at the club.

After beginning his professional career with West Ham United, Andy was signed by Alf Ramsey in May 1959 and made his debut against Huddersfield Town on the opening day of the 1959/60 season.

During the 1960 close-season, Andy took over the captaincy from Reg Pickett and in his first season as skipper, he led the club to the Division Two championship. He was an ever-present the following season when he achieved the ultimate honour of lifting the Division One trophy.

His career at Portman Road lasted until 1964 when he joined Leyton Orient, and after a spell with Plymouth Argyle, he moved into management, first with Gillingham and then Charlton Athletic.

Andy was inducted into the Ipswich Town Hall of Fame in 2011.

DIVISION ONE

31 MARCH 1962		P	W	D	L	F	A	GA	P
1	Ipswich Town	36	21	6	9	83	58	1.431	48
2	Burnley	32	20	6	6	95	54	1.759	46
3	Tottenham Hotspur	34	16	8	10	68	58	1.172	40
4	Everton	34	16	7	11	67	45	1.489	39
5	Sheffield United	34	16	7	11	48	55	0.873	39
6	West Ham United	35	15	8	12	63	67	0.940	38
7	Aston Villa	35	15	7	13	47	45	1.044	37
8	Blackpool	35	13	10	12	59	56	1.054	36
9	Sheffield Wednesday	33	14	6	13	55	44	1.250	34
10	Blackburn Rovers	33	12	10	11	41	42	0.976	34
11	Manchester City	35	14	6	15	68	70	0.971	34
12	Arsenal	33	12	9	12	53	53	1.000	33
13	West Bromwich Albion	36	10	12	14	65	63	1.032	32
14	Manchester United	33	12	8	13	55	58	0.948	32
15	Wolverhampton Wanderers	36	12	8	16	62	71	0.873	32
16	Birmingham City	35	12	8	15	51	68	0.750	32
17	Leicester City	34	13	5	16	54	54	1.000	31
18	Nottingham Forest	35	11	9	15	55	64	0.859	31
19	Bolton Wanderers	34	12	7	15	49	58	0.845	31
20	Cardiff City	34	7	13	14	38	58	0.655	27
21	Fulham	33	9	6	18	49	60	0.817	24
22	Chelsea	35	9	6	20	54	78	0.692	24

Thoughts of winning the league were tempered somewhat by the fact that Burnley now had four games in hand due to FA Cup commitments and postponements and were still considered favourites for the title by most independent pundits. Nevertheless, confidence was high as Ramsey took his men up to Old Trafford to face Manchester United only to see them suffer a humiliating 5-0 defeat with the Red Devils star forward Albert Quixall grabbing a brilliant hat-trick.

With only five games remaining Town had now slipped back to second place, but a week later they managed to get back to winning ways with a narrow 1-0 victory over Cardiff City at Portman Road. The only goal of the game came midway through the first half when City 'keeper Dwyer misjudged a cross allowing Crawford to head goalwards and give Moran the simple task of slotting the ball home from close range.

For their next game, Town welcomed Arsenal to Portman Road for a game that saw the ground's attendance top 30,000 for the first time ever. The game itself started as a pretty dour encounter with all the action coming after the break with the visitors racing to a two-goal lead with strikes from McLeod and then a brilliant overhead kick from Eastham.

At this stage things were really looking bleak for the home side, but Neill gave them a chance to get back into the game when he brought down Crawford in the box allowing Phillips to step up and hammer the ball into the net in typical fashion.

The goal sparked amazing scenes as the crowd spilled over from the packed terraces to race onto the pitch in celebration. Now with their tails up and the fans roaring them on, the home side surged forward, but found the Gunners 'keeper Jack Kelsey in brilliant form making a string of outstanding saves.

Soon afterwards, Phillips sent in a thunderous 20-yard shot which looked a goal all the away only for the ball to strike the crossbar and rebound to safety. Then, with only minutes remaining, Town's pressure finally paid off with Leadbetter forcing the ball home from close range to signal a repeat of the earlier scenes of celebration.

It had been a great comeback by Ramsey's team and the draw saw them move level on points with Burnley who were now only managing to hang on to top spot through their superior goal average.

Amazingly in the next game, away to relegation threatened Chelsea at Stamford Bridge, Town were forced to come back from a two-goal deficit to salvage a point. After goals from Brabrook and Bridges had given the home side an interval lead, Crawford brought Town back into the game with a fine header from a pin-point Leadbetter cross. Then, with fifteen minutes remaining, Mortimer punched away Crawford's goal-bound effort allowing Phillips to send the resultant spot-kick screaming into the net. Chelsea battled hard in the closing stages, but were unable to breach the Ipswich defence and were forced to settle for a draw, a result that saw them relegated from the top flight for the first time in thirty-two years.

For their penultimate game of the season and with the title race on a knife-edge, Ipswich travelled to London to face Arsenal at Highbury for what many were describing as a must win game. If ever Alf Ramsey needed a big performance from his team to keep their title hopes alive, then this was it.

A crowd of just under 45,000 packed the North London ground and the vast majority were stunned into silence after only fifteen minutes when Phillips rose to send a looping header over Kelsey and into the net. Soon afterwards, Town doubled their advantage when Crawford fired home from a narrow angle to send the travelling Ipswich fans into sheer ecstacy. After the break Arsenal came more into the game, but Town's points were safe when Crawford netted arguably his best goal of the season, brilliantly beating two defenders before firing a terrific shot past Kelsey.

RAY
CRAWFORD

RAY CRAWFORD OPENS THE SCORING AGAINST ASTON VILLA WITH A DIVING HEADER AFTER ELSWORTHY'S HEADER HAD HIT THE BAR

RAY CRAWFORD

PLAYER PROFILE

DATE OF BIRTH:	**13 July 1936**
PLACE OF BIRTH:	**Portsmouth**
IPSWICH TOWN (ALL COMPS):	**353 Appearances · 227 Goals**
1961/62 (LEAGUE ONLY):	**41 Appearances · 33 Goals**

Ray Crawford first came to prominence as a youngster playing for Portsmouth Schoolboys and later for the Combined Services team during his National Service.

Ray served in Malaysia which later earned him the nickname 'jungle boy' among fans. He signed as a professional for Portsmouth in October 1956 and made his Pompey debut on the opening day of the 1957/58 season. A centre-forward with a keen eye for goal, Ray scored nine goals in just 19 games before his progress was halted when he sustained a broken ankle, which kept him on the sidelines for three months.

It was early in the 1958/59 season that Alf Ramsey made his move to land the Portsmouth striker for what quickly turned out to be a bargain transfer fee of just £6,000. A prolific scorer from the off, Ray's goals, coupled with those of strike partner Ted Phillips, catapulted the team to the Division Two title in 1960/61 when the pair netted an incredible 70 of Town's 100 goals. Ray missed only one game during the 1961/62 Division One championship-winning season, finishing the campaign as top-scorer with 33 league goals and also became the first Ipswich Town player to win full international honours for England.

Ray's career at Portman Road lasted until September 1963 when he joined Wolverhampton Wanderers in a £40,000 deal. A spell with West Bromwich Albion followed before he returned to Portman Road in March 1966, staying for another three years before joining Charlton Athletic midway through the 1968/69 season. Ray finished his playing career in English football with Colchester Utd, famously scoring two of the goals in their 3-2 victory over Leeds United in the FA Cup in 1971. He then had a spell out in South Africa playing for Durban City before returning home to enjoy a number of years in coaching, first with Brighton and Hove Albion and later back at Portsmouth where he began his career.

One of the all-time greats at Portman Road, his haul of 227 goals in 353 appearances remains a club record, and in 2007 he became one of five inaugural members to be inducted into the Ipswich Town Hall of Fame. **49**

The result meant Town were now two points clear at the top as they went into the final game at home to Aston Villa. However, with Burnley having a game in hand and a superior goal average, most pundits still rated the men from Turf Moor as title favourites, particularly bearing in mind that their next game was at home to already-relegated Chelsea.

Prior to the game at Portman Road, Aston Villa manager Joe Mercer had thrown down the gauntlet predicting that his team would not only beat Ipswich, but also that Burnley were certainties for the title. For long periods in an afternoon of high drama and tension, the Villa boss's prediction appeared to be coming true as Town laboured to find a way through the visitor's resolute defence.

Chances were few and far between with Villa beginning to look the more likely winners and as the game approached the final quarter the home fans could see their team's title chances slipping away.

Then, on 72 minutes, Town won a free-kick out on the right after Baxter had been fouled and when Stephenson floated the ball in, Elsworthy rose to send a looping header goalwards. The effort beat Sims' despairing dive, hit the face of the crossbar, and dropped perfectly for Crawford to run in and send a diving header into the net.

Unprecedented scenes followed as delirious fans poured onto the pitch in celebration and it took the referee some minutes to restore order. Amazingly, a few minutes later, the scenes were repeated after Crawford seized onto a loose ball to double Town's advantage and make the game safe with a terrific left-foot shot.

At the final whistle, the Ipswich players were mobbed by hundreds of supporters even though there had been no news on how Burnley had faired in the game against Chelsea. They eventually managed to find their way to the tunnel and were back in the dressing room before the news finally came through that the game at Turf Moor had ended in a goalless draw and the championship was theirs.

The result was immediately announced over the Portman Road loadspeakers prompting unbelievable scenes of joyous celebration among supporters both young and old. Back in the dressing room champagne flowed freely, most of it supplied by BBC commentator Kenneth Wolstenholme in settlement of a wager he'd had with the Ipswich players when he predicted that Spurs would pip Town for the title.

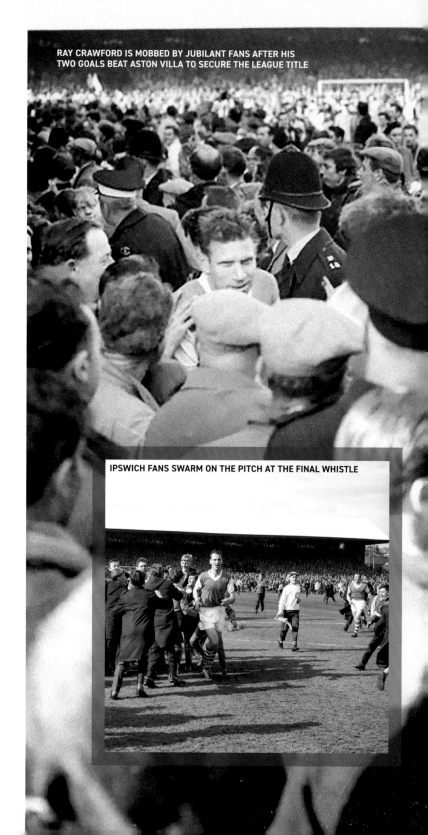

RAY CRAWFORD IS MOBBED BY JUBILANT FANS AFTER HIS TWO GOALS BEAT ASTON VILLA TO SECURE THE LEAGUE TITLE

IPSWICH FANS SWARM ON THE PITCH AT THE FINAL WHISTLE

LET THE CELEBRATIONS BEGIN

THE DREAM BECOMES REALITY

HAIL THE CHAMPIONS
WELL PLAYED
IPSWICH TOWN

INTERFLORA

Unfortunately, the traditional presentation of the trophy and parade through the town had to be put on hold as the Ipswich squad headed off on a pre-arranged continental tour, but when they returned, there were unprecedented scenes as a specially decorated team bus inched through the massive crowds to Cornhill where skipper Andy Nelson hoisted the trophy aloft.

The impossible dream had happened: Ipswich Town, a small-town club who had only been elected to the Football League some 24 years earlier, had lifted the English game's most coveted prize at the first time of asking.

Interviewed afterwards, Alf Ramsey was typically modest saying:

"I'm delighted for everyone associated with the club. I've been lucky to get no serious injuries and we did well because we practice, practice, practice. All weaknesses, the opposition's and ours, are examined and discussed."

Not surprisingly, Ramsey's managerial style was now beginning to attract admiring glances from throughout the English game and it came as no surprise when, in October 1962, the Football Association invited him to succeed Walter Winterbottom as England manager.

Four years later, in 1966, he achieved the ultimate glory when his team were crowned World Champions for the first time ever and a year later his achievements in the game were recognised when he received a knighthood. He remains one of the greatest managers in the history of the game and will always be loved by everyone associated with Ipswich Town where his memory is preserved with a wonderful statue outside Portman Road.

THE CHAMPIONS ARE GREETED BY THOUSANDS
OF ADORING FANS AS THEY ARRIVE ON THE CORNHILL

KEN MALCOLM

PLAYER PROFILE

DATE OF BIRTH:	**25 July 1926**
PLACE OF BIRTH:	**Aberdeen**
IPSWICH TOWN (ALL COMPS):	**291 Appearances · 2 goals**
1961/62 (LEAGUE ONLY):	**3 Appearances**

Signed from Arbroath in May 1954, Ken Malcolm quickly became established as a first-team regular wearing the number three shirt with some distinction throughout the 1950s.

A dependable and consistent tough-tackling defender, Ken was a hugely popular player at Portman Road, eventually going on to make almost 300 appearances for the club in a lengthy career during which he picked up Division Three (South) and Division Two championship medals, Sadly however, he only managed to play the first three games of the 1961/62 season when a leg injury, followed by a severe bout of sciatica, saw him miss the remainder of the campaign.

In his absence, John Compton took over the number three shirt and his outstanding performances meant that Ken played only eighteen more times for Town before retiring from the game at the end of the 1963/64 season.

He then joined the Portman Road backroom staff helping manager Jackie Milburn set up the youth system that would produce so many great players in the years ahead. Ken died in May 2006 aged 79.

JOHN COMPTON

PLAYER PROFILE

DATE OF BIRTH:	**27 August 1937**
PLACE OF BIRTH:	**Poplar, East London**
IPSWICH TOWN (ALL COMPS):	**131 Appearances**
1961/62 (LEAGUE ONLY):	**39 Appearances**

The eldest of a family of five, John Compton was born in Poplar, East London and joined Chelsea at the age of sixteen.

He made his league debut in a Division One fixture at Blackpool a little over a year later, but was very much a fringe player in the years that followed and in July 1960, he was signed by Alf Ramsey for a modest fee of £4,000. Although he made his first-team debut in the 1960/61 season, it was the following campaign that John became an established first-team player after being drafted into the side to replace regular right-back Ken Malcolm who suffered a serious back injury in the third game of the season.

Originally a midfield player, John adapted brilliantly to his new role, playing in every one of the remaining 39 games of the Division One championship-winning season.

His Portman Road career spanned four years before he moved to Bournemouth at the end of the 1963/64 season. Now retired and still living in the south-coast resort, John was inducted into the Ipswich Town Hall of Fame in 2011.

WE ARE THE CHAMPIONS

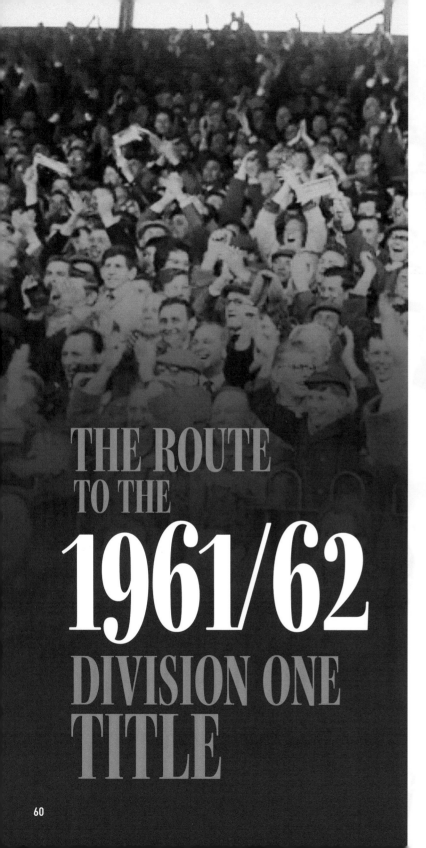

BOLTON WANDERERS 0
IPSWICH TOWN 0

DATE: Saturday 19 August 1961

VENUE: Burnden Park **ATTENDANCE:** 16,708

TOWN TEAM: Bailey, Malcolm, Carberry, Baxter, Elsworthy, Nelson, Stephenson, Moran, Crawford, Phillips, Leadbetter.

BURNLEY 4
Pointer, Harris, Miller, McIlroy.

IPSWICH TOWN 3
Phillips 2, Crawford.

DATE: Tuesday 22 August 1961

VENUE: Turf Moor **ATTENDANCE:** 24,577

TOWN TEAM: Bailey, Carberry, Malcolm, Elsworthy, Nelson, Baxter, Stephenson, Moran, Crawford, Phillips, Leadbetter.

IPSWICH TOWN 2
Betts (og), Leadbetter.

MANCHESTER CITY 4
Barlow, Hayes, Dobing 2.

DATE: Saturday 26 August 1961

VENUE: Portman Road **ATTENDANCE:** 21,473

TOWN TEAM: Bailey, Carberry, Malcolm, Elsworthy, Nelson, Baxter, Stephenson, Moran, Crawford, Phillips, Leadbetter.

IPSWICH TOWN 6
Crawford 2, Stephenson, Moran, Phillips, Leadbetter.

BURNLEY 2
McIlroy, Elsworthy (og).

DATE: Tuesday 29 August 1961

VENUE: Portman Road **ATTENDANCE:** 23,835

TOWN TEAM: Bailey, Carberry, Compton, Elsworthy, Nelson, Baxter, Stephenson, Moran, Crawford, Phillips, Leadbetter.

WEST BROMWICH ALBION 1

Jackson.

IPSWICH TOWN 3

Moran 2, Crawford.

DATE: Saturday 2 September 1961

VENUE: The Hawthorns   **ATTENDANCE:** 19,016

TOWN TEAM: Bailey, Carberry, Compton, Elsworthy, Nelson, Baxter, Stephenson, Moran, Crawford, Phillips, Leadbetter.

IPSWICH TOWN 2

Stephenson, Phillips.

BLACKBURN ROVERS 1

Douglas (pen).

DATE: Tuesday 5 September 1961

VENUE: Portman Road   **ATTENDANCE:** 24,928

TOWN TEAM: Bailey, Carberry, Compton, Elsworthy, Nelson, Baxter, Stephenson, Moran, Crawford, Phillips, Leadbetter.

IPSWICH TOWN 4

Crawford, Phillips 2, Moran.

BIRMINGHAM CITY 1

Singer.

DATE: Saturday 9 September 1961

VENUE: Portman Road   **ATTENDANCE:** 20,017

TOWN TEAM: Bailey, Carberry, Compton, Elsworthy, Nelson, Baxter, Stephenson, Moran, Crawford, Phillips, Leadbetter.

EVERTON 5

Temple 3, Young, Bingham.

IPSWICH TOWN 2

Phillips, Moran.

DATE: Saturday 16 September 1961

VENUE: Goodison Park   **ATTENDANCE:** 35,259

TOWN TEAM: Hall, Carberry, Compton, Baxter, Nelson, Elsworthy, Stephenson, Moran, Crawford, Phillips, Leadbetter.

BLACKBURN ROVERS 2

Lawther, McEvoy.

IPSWICH TOWN 2

Phillips 2 (1 pen).

DATE: Monday 18 September 1961

VENUE: Ewood Park   **ATTENDANCE:** 19,904

TOWN TEAM: Hall, Carberry, Compton, Nelson, Elsworthy, Baxter, Stephenson, Moran, Crawford, Phillips, Leadbetter.

IPSWICH TOWN 2

Crawford 2.

FULHAM 4

Cook, Cohen, Haynes, O'Connell.

DATE: Saturday 23 September 1961

VENUE: Portman Road   **ATTENDANCE:** 23,050

TOWN TEAM: Hall, Carberry, Compton, Baxter, Nelson, Elsworthy, Stephenson, Moran, Crawford, Phillips, Leadbetter.

SHEFFIELD WEDNESDAY 1

Fantham.

IPSWICH TOWN 4

Phillips 2, Crawford, Leadbetter.

DATE: Saturday 30 September 1961

VENUE: Hillsborough   **ATTENDANCE:** 26,565

TOWN TEAM: Hall, Carberry, Compton, Baxter, Nelson, Elsworthy, Stephenson, Moran, Crawford, Phillips, Leadbetter.

IPSWICH TOWN 4

Crawford 2, Phillips 2.

WEST HAM UNITED 2

Sealey, Musgrove.

DATE: Saturday 7 October 1961

VENUE: Portman Road   **ATTENDANCE:** 28,059

TOWN TEAM: Bailey, Carberry, Compton, Baxter, Nelson, Elsworthy, Stephenson, Moran, Crawford, Phillips, Leadbetter.

SHEFFIELD UNITED 2

Russell, Pace.

IPSWICH TOWN 1

Leadbetter.

DATE: Saturday 14 October 1961

VENUE: Bramall Lane **ATTENDANCE:** 22,194

TOWN TEAM: Bailey, Carberry, Compton, Baxter, Nelson, Elsworthy, Stephenson, Moran, Crawford, Phillips, Leadbetter.

IPSWICH TOWN 3

Phillips, Crawford 2.

TOTTENHAM HOTSPUR 2

Cliff Jones.

DATE: Saturday 21 October 1961

VENUE: Portman Road **ATTENDANCE:** 28,778

TOWN TEAM: Bailey, Carberry, Compton, Baxter, Nelson, Elsworthy, Stephenson, Moran, Crawford, Phillips, Leadbetter.

BLACKPOOL 1

Parry.

IPSWICH TOWN 1

Phillips.

DATE: Saturday 28 October 1961

VENUE: Bloomfield Road **ATTENDANCE:** 19,773

TOWN TEAM: Bailey, Carberry, Compton, Baxter, Nelson, Elsworthy, Stephenson, Moran, Crawford, Phillips, Leadbetter.

IPSWICH TOWN 1

Phillips.

NOTTINGHAM FOREST 0

DATE: Saturday 4 November 1961

VENUE: Portman Road **ATTENDANCE:** 19,068

TOWN TEAM: Bailey, Carberry, Compton, Baxter, Nelson, Elsworthy, Stephenson, Moran, Crawford, Phillips, Leadbetter.

WOLVERHAMPTON WANDERERS 2

Wharton, Hinton.

IPSWICH TOWN 0

DATE: Saturday 11 November 1961

VENUE: Molineux **ATTENDANCE:** 21,711

TOWN TEAM: Bailey, Carberry, Compton, Baxter, Nelson, Elsworthy, Stephenson, Moran, Crawford, Phillips, Leadbetter.

IPSWICH TOWN 4

Phillips 2, Crawford, Elsworthy.

MANCHESTER UNITED 1

McMillan.

DATE: Saturday 18 November 1961

VENUE: Portman Road **ATTENDANCE:** 25,755

TOWN TEAM: Bailey, Carberry, Compton, Baxter, Nelson, Elsworthy, Curtis, Moran, Crawford, Phillips, Leadbetter.

CARDIFF CITY 0

IPSWICH TOWN 3

Phillips 2, Moran.

DATE: Saturday 25 November 1961

VENUE: Ninian Park **ATTENDANCE:** 22,823

TOWN TEAM: Bailey, Carberry, Compton, Baxter, Nelson, Elsworthy, Stephenson, Moran, Crawford, Phillips, Leadbetter.

IPSWICH TOWN 5

Crawford 3, Moran, Stephenson.

CHELSEA 2

Tambling, Murray.

DATE: Saturday 2 December 1961

VENUE: Portman Road **ATTENDANCE:** 22,726

TOWN TEAM: Bailey, Carberry, Compton, Baxter, Nelson, Elsworthy, Stephenson, Moran, Crawford, Phillips, Leadbetter.

ASTON VILLA 3

McParland 2, Thomson.

IPSWICH TOWN 0

DATE: Saturday 9 December 1961

VENUE: Villa Park   **ATTENDANCE:** 31,924

TOWN TEAM: Bailey, Carberry, Compton, Baxter, Nelson, Elsworthy, Stephenson, Moran, Crawford, Phillips, Leadbetter.

IPSWICH TOWN 2

Crawford 2.

BOLTON WANDERERS 1

Holden.

DATE: Saturday 16 December 1961

VENUE: Portman Road   **ATTENDANCE:** 16,587

TOWN TEAM: Bailey, Carberry, Compton, Baxter, Nelson, Elsworthy, Stephenson, Moran, Crawford, Phillips, Leadbetter.

MANCHESTER CITY 3

Hayes, Dobing, Young.

IPSWICH TOWN 0

DATE: Saturday 23 December 1961

VENUE: Maine Road   **ATTENDANCE:** 18,376

TOWN TEAM: Bailey, Carberry, Compton, Baxter, Nelson, Elsworthy, Stephenson, Moran, Crawford, Phillips, Leadbetter.

IPSWICH TOWN 1

Crawford.

LEICESTER CITY 0

DATE: Tuesday 26 December 1961

VENUE: Portman Road   **ATTENDANCE:** 18,146

TOWN TEAM: Bailey, Carberry, Compton, Baxter, Nelson, Elsworthy, Stephenson, Moran, Crawford, Phillips, Owen.

IPSWICH TOWN 3

Stephenson, Moran, Leadbetter.

WEST BROMWICH ALBION 0

DATE: Saturday 13 January 1962

VENUE: Portman Road   **ATTENDANCE:** Attendance: 18,378

TOWN TEAM: Bailey, Carberry, Compton, Baxter, Nelson, Elsworthy, Stephenson, Moran, Crawford, Phillips, Leadbetter.

BIRMINGHAM CITY 3

Leek 2, Baxter (og).

IPSWICH TOWN 1

Crawford.

DATE: Saturday 20 January 1962

VENUE: St. Andrews   **ATTENDANCE:** 26,968

TOWN TEAM: Hall, Carberry, Compton, Baxter, Nelson, Elsworthy, Stephenson, Moran, Crawford, Phillips, Leadbetter.

IPSWICH TOWN 4

Phillips, Moran, Elsworthy, Crawford.

EVERTON 2

Bingham, Harris.

DATE: Saturday 3 February 1962

VENUE: Portman Road   **ATTENDANCE:** 22,572

TOWN TEAM: Bailey, Carberry, Compton, Baxter, Nelson, Elsworthy, Stephenson, Moran, Crawford, Phillips, Leadbetter.

FULHAM 1

Mullery.

IPSWICH TOWN 2

Stephenson, Crawford.

DATE: Saturday 10 February 1962

VENUE: Craven Cottage   **ATTENDANCE:** 25,209

TOWN TEAM: Bailey, Carberry, Compton, Baxter, Nelson, Elsworthy, Stephenson, Moran, Crawford, Phillips, Leadbetter.

CHAMPIONS
OF ENGLAND

CAPTAIN ANDY NELSON HOLDS THE CHAMPIONSHIP TROPHY ALOFT

ROY STEPHENSON

PLAYER PROFILE

DATE OF BIRTH:	**27 May 1932**
PLACE OF BIRTH:	**Crook**
IPSWICH TOWN (ALL COMPS):	**163 Appearances · 26 Goals**
1961/62 (LEAGUE ONLY):	**41 Appearances · 7 Goals**

Born in Crook, County Durham, Roy Stephenson began his career with Burnley, joining the Lancashire club as a sixteen-year-old before progressing to the first team and eventually going on to make over 100 Division One appearances for 'The Clarets'.

Roy then had spells with Rotherham United, Blackburn Rovers and Leicester City before being signed by Alf Ramsey in July 1960. A right-winger with pace, power and the ability to deliver pin-point crosses, he helped Town clinch the Division Two title in his first season and missed only one game during the following campaign when they were crowned Football League champions.

Roy stayed at Portman Road until June 1965 when he signed for Eastern Counties League side Lowestoft Town and he continued to live in Ipswich until his death in February 2000, aged 67.

In 2009 he was inducted into the Ipswich Town Hall of Fame.

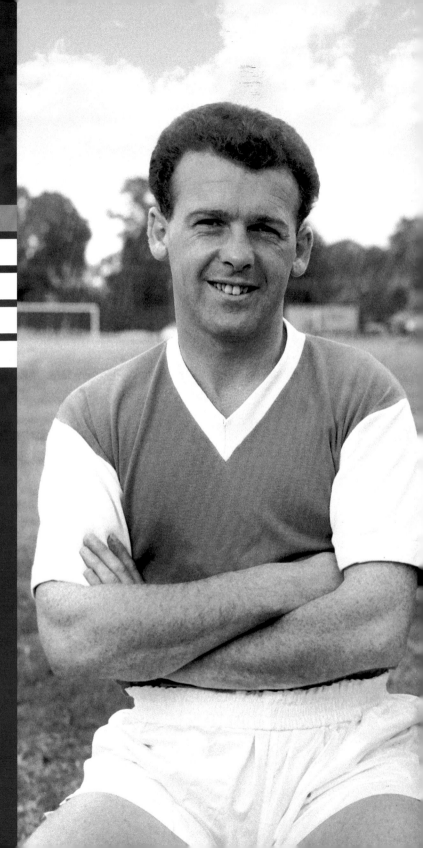

DOUG MORAN

PLAYER PROFILE

DATE OF BIRTH:	**29 July 1934**
PLACE OF BIRTH:	**Musselburgh**
IPSWICH TOWN (ALL COMPS):	**123 Appearances · 37 Goals**
1961/62 (LEAGUE ONLY):	**42 Appearances · 14 Goals**

A record £12,000 signing from Falkirk, Doug Moran was Alf Ramsey's only addition to Town's 1960/61 Division Two Championship-winning side.

Highly rated by the Ipswich boss, Doug was an ever-present in the Ipswich team that lifted the Division One title in 1962 netting 14 goals, an impressive return for a midfield player.

He began his top-class playing career with Hibernian before joining Falkirk and in his first season he picked up a Scottish Cup winners' medal after netting the winning goal against Kilmarnock at Hampden Park.

Doug's Ipswich Town career lasted until 1964 when he headed back to Scotland to join Dundee United before returning to Falkirk for a second spell with the club. He brought his playing career to end with a short spell at Cowdenbeath before finally hanging up his boots at the end of the 1968/69 season. Doug now lives in Inveresk, East Lothian and in 2011 he was inducted into the Ipswich Town Hall of Fame.

WEST HAM UNITED 2

Dick, Kirkup.

IPSWICH TOWN 2

Leadbetter, Phillips (pen).

DATE: Saturday 24 February 1962

VENUE: Upton Park   **ATTENDANCE:** 27,763

TOWN TEAM: Bailey, Carberry, Compton, Baxter, Nelson, Elsworthy, Stephenson, Moran, Crawford, Phillips, Leadbetter.

IPSWICH TOWN 4

Moran, Leadbetter, Crawford 2.

SHEFFIELD UNITED 0

DATE: Saturday 3 March 1962

VENUE: Portman Road   **ATTENDANCE:** 20,158

TOWN TEAM: Bailey, Carberry, Compton, Baxter, Nelson, Elsworthy, Stephenson, Moran, Crawford, Phillips, Leadbetter.

IPSWICH TOWN 2

Crawford, Stephenson.

SHEFFIELD WEDNESDAY 1

Dobson.

DATE: Friday 9 March 1962

VENUE: Portman Road   **ATTENDANCE:** 23,713

TOWN TEAM: Bailey, Carberry, Compton, Baxter, Nelson, Elsworthy, Stephenson, Moran, Crawford, Phillips, Leadbetter.

TOTTENHAM HOTSPUR 1

Greaves.

IPSWICH TOWN 3

Crawford, Phillips 2.

DATE: Wednesday 14 March 1962

VENUE: White Hart Lane   **ATTENDANCE:** 51,098

TOWN TEAM: Bailey, Carberry, Compton, Baxter, Nelson, Elsworthy, Stephenson, Moran, Crawford, Phillips, Leadbetter.

IPSWICH TOWN 1

Moran.

BLACKPOOL 1

Charnley.

DATE: Saturday 17 March 1962

VENUE: Portman Road   **ATTENDANCE:** 22,450

TOWN TEAM: Bailey, Carberry, Compton, Baxter, Nelson, Elsworthy, Stephenson, Moran, Crawford, Phillips, Leadbetter.

NOTTINGHAM FOREST 1

Julians.

IPSWICH TOWN 1

Moran.

DATE: Saturday 24 March 1962

VENUE: City Ground   **ATTENDANCE:** 26,053

TOWN TEAM: Bailey, Carberry, Compton, Baxter, Nelson, Elsworthy, Stephenson, Moran, Crawford, Curtis, Leadbetter.

LEICESTER CITY 0

IPSWICH TOWN 2

Crawford, Stephenson.

DATE: Wednesday 28 March 1962

VENUE: Filbert Street   **ATTENDANCE:** 19,068

TOWN TEAM: Bailey, Carberry, Compton, Pickett, Nelson, Elsworthy, Stephenson, Moran, Crawford, Curtis, Leadbetter.

IPSWICH TOWN 3

Phillips (pen), Crawford, Moran.

WOLVERHAMPTON WANDERERS 2

Flowers, McParland.

DATE: Saturday 31 March 1962

VENUE: Portman Road   **ATTENDANCE:** 23,153

TOWN TEAM: Bailey, Carberry, Compton, Pickett, Nelson, Elsworthy, Stephenson, Moran, Crawford, Phillips, Leadbetter.

MANCHESTER UNITED 5

Quixall 3, Stiles, Setters.

IPSWICH TOWN 0

DATE: Saturday 7 April 1962

VENUE: Old Trafford   **ATTENDANCE:** 24,976

TOWN TEAM: Bailey, Carberry, Compton, Baxter, Nelson, Elsworthy, Stephenson, Moran, Curtis, Phillips, Leadbetter.

IPSWICH TOWN 1

Moran.

CARDIFF CITY 0

DATE: Saturday 14 April 1962

VENUE: Portman Road   **ATTENDANCE:** 17,693

TOWN TEAM: Bailey, Carberry, Compton, Baxter, Nelson, Pickett, Stephenson, Moran, Crawford, Phillips, Leadbetter.

IPSWICH TOWN 2

Phillips (pen), Leadbetter.

ARSENAL 2

MacLeod, Eastham.

DATE: Friday 20 April 1962

VENUE: Portman Road   **ATTENDANCE:** 30,649

TOWN TEAM: Bailey, Carberry, Compton, Baxter, Nelson, Elsworthy, Stephenson, Moran, Crawford, Phillips, Leadbetter.

CHELSEA 2

Brabrook, Bridges.

IPSWICH TOWN 2

Crawford, Phillips (pen).

DATE: Saturday 21 April 1962

VENUE: Stamford Bridge   **ATTENDANCE:** 28,462

TOWN TEAM: Bailey, Carberry, Compton, Baxter, Nelson, Elsworthy, Stephenson, Moran, Crawford, Phillips, Leadbetter.

ARSENAL 0

IPSWICH TOWN 3

Phillips, Crawford 2.

DATE: Monday 23 April 1962

VENUE: Highbury   **ATTENDANCE:** 44,694

TOWN TEAM: Bailey, Carberry, Compton, Baxter, Nelson, Elsworthy, Stephenson, Moran, Crawford, Phillips, Leadbetter.

IPSWICH TOWN 2

Crawford 2.

ASTON VILLA 0

DATE: Saturday 28 April 1962

VENUE: Portman Road   **ATTENDANCE:** 28,932

TOWN TEAM: Bailey, Carberry, Compton, Baxter, Nelson, Elsworthy, Stephenson, Moran, Crawford, Phillips, Leadbetter.

DIVISION ONE									
1 MAY 1962	P	W	D	L	F	A	GA	P
1	**Ipswich Town**	**42**	**24**	**8**	**10**	**93**	**67**	**1.388**	**56**
2	Burnley	42	21	11	10	101	67	1.507	53
3	Tottenham Hotspur	42	21	10	11	88	69	1.275	52
4	Everton	42	20	11	11	88	54	1.630	51
5	Sheffield United	42	19	9	14	61	69	0.884	47
6	Sheffield Wednesday	42	20	6	16	72	58	1.241	46
7	Aston Villa	42	18	8	16	65	56	1.161	44
8	West Ham United	42	17	10	15	76	82	0.927	44
9	West Bromwich Albion	42	15	13	14	83	67	1.239	43
10	Arsenal	42	16	11	15	71	72	0.986	43
11	Bolton Wanderers	42	16	10	16	62	66	0.939	42
12	Manchester City	42	17	7	18	78	81	0.963	41
13	Blackpool	42	15	11	16	70	75	0.933	41
14	Leicester City	42	17	6	19	72	71	1.014	40
15	Manchester United	42	15	9	18	72	75	0.960	39
16	Blackburn Rovers	42	14	11	17	50	58	0.862	39
17	Birmingham City	42	14	10	18	65	81	0.802	38
18	Wolverhampton Wanderers	42	13	10	19	73	86	0.849	36
19	Nottingham Forest	42	13	10	19	63	79	0.797	36
20	Fulham	42	13	7	22	66	74	0.892	33
21	Cardiff City	42	9	14	19	50	81	0.617	32
22	Chelsea	42	9	10	23	63	94	0.670	28

Roll of Honour

THANK YOU TO THE FOLLOWING FANS WHO PRE-ORDERED

Elizabeth Edwards	Robin Upfold	Steve Stagg	Mark Pirrie	Mark Holdaway
Colin Kreidewolf	Gale Rivera	Julian Toop	Steve Wain	Simon Drake
Michael Nevard	Robert Garrett	Richard Townsend	David Jenkins	To Nanna & Grandad
Stephen Nevard	Paul Levermore	Martin Talbot	Ivor Harrison	Robert Laukkanen
Derek Cook	Mark Calver	Rod Gray	James Smith	Thomas Wadsworth
Juian Bentin	Andy Harrison BCTB	David Scotchmer	Nick Moore	Kuen-Wah Cheung
Freddie Maxted	Albert Tweed	Mike and Jill Spink	Charlie Bullock	Mark Wright
Richard F G Smith	Alan Seely	Geoff Pickess	James Eadie	Mike Ager
Raymond Smith	David Andrews	Richard Westrope	Matthew Noble	Damon Shipley
Robin Furber	Roger Whiting	Malcolm Bruce	Chris Farndon	Pamela Robinson
Mark Humphreys	Gordon Page	Albie Davis	James Farndon	Connor Robinson
Brett M. Johnson	Warren Boore	David Wink Peachey	Graham Downey	David Potter
Michael & Bob Martel	Chris Harvey	Martin Page	Stephen Downey	Matthew Chaplin
Fiona Taylor	Geoffrey Mann	Gary Bullock	Paul Jackson	Robert Avis
Harald Haagensen	Chris Butler	Mike Smart	Chris & Wendy Hayes	Sue Baillie
Stephen R. Pike	Tim Bacon	Russell Smith	Tanya	Peter Simpson
Carlton Matthew	Arthur Pope	Andrew K Stevenson	Richard Pack	Jason Jolley
Paul Hart	Terry Cobbold	Kevin Higham	Chris Winger	Mark Wadeson Berry
Tom Tomalin	Sean Lindsay	Archie Hughie & Matt	Michael Kettle	Tim Stovell
Harry Nicholl	Phil Lawes	Andrew Norton	Allez les Bleus!	Jez Grimwood
Charlie Nicholl	Lawrence John	Hugo Plowden	Rosemary Grimsey	Vic Grimwood
Christopher Calver	Shayne Hunt	Craig Alexander	Elizabeth Boggis	Mark James Gray
Richard Ager	Gerry B	Jason Pegelow	Ray Kemp	Brian Haward
James Richardson	Rory Henderson	Jim Heathfield	Bernie Soudain	Stuart Watkinson
Stephen M Lockwood	Nigel Hood	David Allison	Dale Osborne	Andrew Dowse
Daniel Seabourne	Jim Savage	Jason Tom Beckett	Philip Jessup	Michael W Good
Dudley Diaper	Trevor Bishop	Anton Smurf Foulger	John Pearson	Norman Peck
Barry Jessup	Mark Mcfarlane	Derek Ling	Tim Beecroft	Melvin Hines
Izaak Morley Jessup	Paul Bailey	Richard Carter	Mark Bullard	Stephen Botwright
Howard Beaumont	Kean Silvester	John Thompson	Michael Allen	Colin Bones
Mick Dye	Beryl Vincent	Andrew Sawyer	Kate Parker	Paul 'Wack' Peachey
Ian 'Chunky' Flack	Tony Cox	John Marney	David Dickinson	Richard Casburn

David Camp	Adam Tanner	Bubba Huffey	Jonathan Bloomfield	Simon Thorpe
Julie Tunney	Colin Webb	Mervyn Russen	Nigel Woody Woodmason	Jamie Bloyce
Steven Burgess	Heather Webb	Michael Rowley	Adam Woody Woodmason	Phil Bullen
Simon Sheppard	Brett Mickelburgh	Jonathan Beatton	Harry and Dalia	Michael Oliver
Mary Carlill	Brett Mansell	Michael Alcock	Alasdair Ross	Richard Lord
Graham Wren	Frank Partridge	Mark Leeks	Iain Jack	Tony Farrow
Paul Edward Bradley	Billy Robinson	Paul Holden	Bryn Thomas	Damian Pye
Shaun Ellingham	Ivan Boreham	Kevin Filby	David Groom	Emerson Fairweather
John May	Darran Paddy	Joe Fairs	Neil P. Ross	Richard Leeks
John R Berry	Geoff Horrex	Crumpton Clarke	David Chadwick	Kelvin Sherman
David Double	Dan March	Stephen Foster	Bill Hone	Nigel King
Donald Flory	Ben Jones	Chris Fleet	Steve Artiss	Neil Williams
Andy Hogg	Ian Burch	Graham Turner	John Goode	Brian Scott
Simon Topper	Christine Barned	Ted Clarke	Adrian Sherman	Arthur Moir
Brian Rayner	Matt Moore	Simon Aldred	Bob & Martine Porter	Jo Whatling
Marc/Bern Brinkley	Helen Cairns	Mark & Isaac Haynes	Barry Richardson	Alan
Colin "the Goat" Plumb	Damian (040712) Junior	Dennis Cyrille	Stephen Curtis	Barry Lambert
Glenn Sedgwick	George Lawrence	Chris Deal	Craig Finbow	Steven Dowe
The Roper Family	Stephen Fewkes	Denise Hammond	Andrew Roberts	Glenn Ash
John Rodas	Dexter Amos	Maurice Ashton	Mark Turner	Phil and Wendy Bloom
Graham Gunn	Paul "Cookie" Cook	Ian Taylor	Gary French	Tim Kenny
To Dad Love Brook	Mark Taylor	Lee Forsdyke	Mark & William Hunt	Peter Lord
Michael Rose	Colin Taylor	Geoff Cook	David...RFATOWNFAN	Wesley Stankiewicz
Neil Johnson	Barry Ford	Jack Garnham	Roy Crook	Paul Adams
William Palfreman	David Hart	Jackie Grant	Richard Woodward	Ron Green
Michael Bicker	Roy Bruce	Phil Hanks	Seb Brown	Nigel Richard Nunn
James Bunn	Grant Smith	Brian Brinkley	Paul Atkinson	Jeff Norman
Lord Philip C Harris	Matthew Becker	Keith & Dean Lomax	Terry Bates	Peter & Mandy Garner
Lord Andrew K Harris	Mike Wright	Steven P Reynolds	Robert Mutimer	Michael Scutcher
Andy Astle	Ashley Martin	Tim Love	Ben Doyle	Stephen Prentice
Dean Roseman	Hayden Martin	James Ager	Steven Farthing	Neil Prentice
Ronald Harvey	Michael Hugman	Horry Money	Grahame Cryer	Matt Newman
Chris Burke	Linda&Brian Woodrow	Scott LeDieu	Charlie Clarke	Richard Jarrett
Jags Singh	Ron Green	Ed Groenhart	Shaun Cobbold	Billy King
John Maplestone	John A. Chambers RIP	Steve Waters	Martin Stonebridge	John Fenton

ACKNOWLEDGEMENTS

This publication would not have been possible without the wealth of information discovered while on this title-winning footballing journey. Also, it is important to state that certain statistics and details are not universally agreed upon. In such instances I have used my best judgement, but then, this book is primarily a celebration of an exceptional season in the history of Ipswich Town Football Club and aims to excite and inspire Town fans of all ages, and in the case of some, bring some great memories and emotions flooding back.

I wish to express my thanks to Elizabeth Edwards and Colin Kreidewolf for their help and acknowledge the following sources, all of which I have referred to in varying degrees:

www.prideofanglia.com
The Men Who Made the Town, John Eastwood and Tony Moyse (up until 1984/85)
Suffolk Punch, Ipswich Town FC 1936-96, edited by Tony Moyse
Ipswich Town Supporters Annual 1992/93
John Lyall: A Life in Football, by Dr. Phil Stevens
Ipswich Town The Modern Era - a complete record by Rob Hadgraft
The PFA Premier League and Football League players records 1946-2005

A big thank you to you all! Dedicated to all Town fans, past, present and future

SECOND DIVISION 1991/92

CHAMPIONS

IPSWICH TOWN FOOTBALL CLUB

Written by Brian Leng
Statistics compiled by Chris Leng

a twocan publication

©2021. Published by twocan under licence from Ipswich Town FC.

ISBN: 978-1-913362-91-1

50 ANNIVERSARY

PICTURES:
Action Images, Alamy, East Anglian Daily Times, Press Association & Ipswich Town FC.

MICK MILLS AND BOBBY ROBSON WITH THE 1981 UEFA CUP

BOBBY FERGUSON

When Ipswich Town lifted the UEFA Cup in 1981, Bobby Robson's star-studded team appeared to be on the verge of becoming established as one of the top sides in European football.

After the disappointment of being knocked out in the first round of the following season's UEFA Cup to Alex Ferguson's Aberdeen, 1981/82 turned out to be another great campaign, with the Blues finishing second in the League, reaching the fifth round of the FA Cup and the semi-finals of the League Cup.

However, things can change quickly in football and during the 1983 pre-season, the news broke that Robson had been offered the England manager's job. Ironically, just as they had done with Alf Ramsey almost exactly twenty years earlier, the Football Association managed to persuade the Town boss to sever his ties with the club and take over the national team.

It was, of course, the ultimate accolade for Bobby Robson, but it did leave the Town directors with a major problem in terms of finding a suitable successor for the Portman Road hot-seat. Eventually, hoping to maintain continuity they decided to promote from within by offering the job to Bobby Ferguson, a man who had been coach of the Youth team, then the Reserve team, before moving up to work alongside Robson and the first team.

Liverpool had made a similar appointment when they promoted Bob Paisley following Bill Shankly's retirement, a move that saw an almost seamless transition. Ferguson's appointment certainly made a lot of sense given that he knew the players well having worked with the vast majority since they had joined the club as youngsters.

However, before a ball had been kicked in the 1982/83 season Town's new boss suffered a major blow when star midfielder Arnold Muhren decided to sever his ties with the club and join Manchester United. The season would also see the departure of Mick Mills to Southampton and Alan Brazil who joined Spurs for £425,000. Predictably, losing players of such quality dispelled any hopes of a title challenge, although Ferguson's first season in charge saw Town finish in a respectable ninth place.

The following campaign began without Dutch international midfield star Frans Thijssen who had moved to Vancouver Whitecaps and he would later be followed by Paul Mariner who joined Arsenal and John Wark who headed north to Liverpool.

3

Bobby Robson's all-conquering team was now being slowly dismantled, and any hopes of European football returning to Portman Road were now little more than a pipe-dream. Now, First Division survival was the main cause for concern and the 1984/85 season saw the side finish in a precarious 17th position, just one point above the drop zone.

After Russell Osman left the club during the 1985/86 pre-season, followed by George Burley just a few games into the campaign, things were on the slide. When Ferguson took his team to Sheffield Wednesday for the final game of the season, they needed a point to avoid the drop. Sadly, a single goal defeat consigned Ipswich Town back to Division Two after eighteen years in the top flight.

Surprisingly, the Ipswich board decided to remain loyal to Bobby Ferguson giving him the opportunity to take the club back to the top flight at first attempt. They were now without their legendary defender Terry Butcher who had joined Rangers, but a decent campaign saw them reach the play-offs, only to lose narrowly to Charlton Athletic at the semi-final stage.

Predictably perhaps, Ferguson's tenure at the club ended and was soon replaced by John Duncan, a man who had enjoyed an outstanding playing career in the game. Sadly, he faired little better and in his three seasons at the club, he was unable to mount a serious promotion challenge and he was sacked at the end of the 1989/90 season.

Again the search was on for a new manager and after much deliberation the Ipswich board decided to offer the job to John Lyall, a man with vast experience in the game. A West Ham United man through and through, Lyall had served the club, first as a player, then coach and finally as manager for over thirty years.

Capped by England at youth international level, injury brought his playing career to a premature end at the age of only 23 and he then moved into coaching at Upton Park, eventually becoming assistant manager under Ron Greenwood. In 1974, after Ron Greenwood moved upstairs to become West Ham's general manager, Lyall was appointed as the Hammers' new manager, a post he held for almost fifteen years.

GEORGE BURLEY

TERRY BUTCHER

JOHN LYALL AND RON GREENWOOD AT WEMBLEY AFTER THE HAMMERS' FA CUP TRIUMPH

5

JOHN LYALL AND THE WEST HAM DUG-OUT JUBILANT AT THE FINAL WHISTLE AFTER THEIR FA CUP VICTORY OVER ARSENAL

In 1980, Lyall led West Ham to FA Cup glory when they lifted the trophy with a 1-0 victory over red-hot favourites Arsenal at Wembley and the following season promotion back to Division One was achieved.

Highly respected in the game, John Lyall was, apparently, disappointed at the circumstances of his departure from Upton Park in 1989 and was desperate to prove his ability with another crack at management. In May 1990, when Ipswich made their move to secure his services he was, seemingly, very happy working for Tottenham Hotspur as technical advisor to Terry Venables, but keen to begin a new challenge.

At this stage in Lyall's career, a move to East Anglia and Portman Road with its friendly family atmosphere seemed the perfect fit and he was said to proud to add his name to Town's list of celebrated managers.

Town's new boss immediately set about establishing a new management structure at the club by appointing Charlie Woods as his assistant and he then brought in Mick McGiven as first-team coach, a former colleague from Upton Park and a man who would soon become a key figure in the Portman Road backroom staff.

Town began the 1990/91 season without John Wark who had left the club for the second time to join Middlesbrough, although his stay on Teesside would soon turn out to be relatively short-lived.

Defeats in their first two games, a 2-0 loss at home to Sheffield Wednesday and then a single goal reverse at Swindon, didn't auger well for the new boss, but consecutive victories over West Bromwich Albion and Blackburn Rovers helped settle the nerves.

Progress in the transfer market was slow and it was January before Lyall was able to make his first major signings when he secured the services of two former West Ham players, Steve Whitton, a £150,000 buy from Sheffield Wednesday and Paul Goddard from Millwall.

Both were vastly experience players who would turn out to be excellent acquisitions for the club. Nevertheless, Town were never serious promotion candidates during Lyall's first campaign in charge finishing in a disappointing 14th place in Division Two and few could have predicted the incredible success that lay ahead in the forthcoming season.

THE ADVENTURE BEGINS

CHRIS KIWOMYA

When the 1991/92 season got under way. Ipswich Town were ranked very much as outsiders in the Division Two promotion stakes, with the bookmakers quoting odds of 25/1 against John Lyall's team finishing the campaign in top spot with North-East giants Newcastle United and Sunderland ranked as the favourites to lift the title.

Nevertheless, the Town boss was apparently quietly confident that his team could mount a strong promotion challenge as they headed to the West Country to meet Bristol Rovers for the first game of the season, who at the time were ground-sharing with non-league Bath City. Even though Town were missing captain David Linighan who was still recovering from a hernia operation, Lyall's confidence appeared to be fully justified as his team got off to a flying start at Twerton Park, racing to a three-goal lead that appeared to have made the game safe with only twenty-five minutes remaining.

A well-taken goal from Dozzell after only twelve minutes had given them a half-time lead, but immediately after the break, Forrest brought down a young Marcus Stewart, later to play for Town, inside the box to concede a penalty. Fortunately, the Ipswich 'keeper produced a fine save from Alexander's spot kick and within a matter of twenty minutes, goals from Goddard and Stockwell had given the visitor's what appeared to be an unassailable lead. Yet, the home side responded almost immediately, ironically through Stewart and two goals from White in the final fifteen minutes gave the home side an unlikely share of the spoils.

A few days later, Town welcomed Port Vale to Portman Road for the first home game of the season, but a crowd of less than 9,000 was a clear indication of the distinct lack of optimism among their fans. In fact, the attendance was the lowest for any opening game at Portman Road since Town had joined the Football League in 1938.

Nevertheless, the home side managed to send their supporters home happy following a narrow 2-1 victory. Kiwomya opened the scoring on 22 minutes after great work by Goddard and Whitton only for the visitors to draw level before the break through a Walker penalty after Humes had brought down Robin van der Laan.

Town's winner came just after the interval and again it was from the spot after Goddard was upended in the box. Thompson stepped up to take the kick and blasted the ball home giving Vale 'keeper Grew no chance.

9

Next up was another home game, this time against Middlesbrough, one of the more fancied teams in Division Two who were now managed by former Charlton Athletic boss Lennie Lawrence. Town's hopes were boosted by the return of skipper David Linighan and while Johnson hit the post early in the game, the contest quickly developed into something of a dour encounter. The breakthrough came in the 48th minute when Dozzell headed home a Thompson corner before Goddard doubled Town's advantage midway through the half after being set up by Whitton. The visitors did manage to snatch a late consolation goal through Wilkinson, but Town held out for a well-earned victory.

The victory had taken Town to the top of Division Two which boosted confidence for their next game at Blackburn Rovers which amazingly produced their third 2-1 victory in a row. Playing a crisp, passing game, Ipswich were in control from the start and opened the scoring on the half-hour mark with a great finish by Kiwomya. Just after the break Goddard doubled Town's advantage, and it wasn't until the dying seconds that Rovers striker David Speedie managed to scramble home a consolation goal after Gayle's header had rebounded off the bar.

DIVISION TWO

	31 AUGUST 1991	P	W	D	L	F	A	GD	P
1	**Ipswich Town**	**4**	**3**	**1**	**0**	**9**	**6**	**3**	**10**
2	Cambridge United	3	3	0	0	10	6	4	9
3	Middlesbrough	5	3	0	2	7	4	3	9
4	Bristol City	4	2	2	0	5	3	2	8
5	Leicester City	3	2	1	0	4	1	3	7
6	Sunderland	4	2	1	1	7	5	2	7
7	Plymouth Argyle	3	2	0	1	5	5	0	6
8	Tranmere Rovers	3	1	2	0	6	4	2	5
9	Wolverhampton Wanderers	3	1	2	0	6	4	2	5
10	Port Vale	5	1	2	2	4	5	-1	5
11	Swindon Town	3	1	1	1	5	4	1	4
12	Derby County	3	1	1	1	4	3	1	4
13	Charlton Athletic	2	1	1	0	3	2	1	4
14	Grimsby Town	3	1	1	1	7	7	0	4
15	Southend United	3	1	1	1	4	4	0	4
16	Portsmouth	3	1	1	1	2	3	-1	4
17	Brighton and Hove Albion	4	1	1	2	6	8	-2	4
18	Newcastle United	4	1	1	2	5	8	-3	4
19	Millwall	3	1	0	2	6	5	1	3
20	Bristol Rovers	3	0	2	1	6	7	-1	2
21	Blackburn Rovers	3	0	1	2	2	4	-2	1
22	Watford	3	0	1	2	3	7	-4	1
23	Barnsley	5	0	1	4	3	10	-7	1
24	Oxford United	3	0	0	3	2	6	-4	0

JASON DOZZELL

PLAYER PROFILE

DATE OF BIRTH:	**9 December 1967**
PLACE OF BIRTH:	**Ipswich**
IPSWICH TOWN (ALL COMPS):	**416 Appearances · 73 Goals**
1991/92 (LEAGUE ONLY):	**45 Appearances · 11 Goals**

Jason Dozzell enjoyed a truly amazing introduction to first-team football when Town boss Bobby Ferguson brought him off the bench to face Coventry City on 4th February 1984.

Not only did he score Town's third goal in a 3-1 victory, but he put himself firmly into the record books being the youngest player to both play and score for Ipswich at the age of only 16 years and 57 days. Incredibly, Jason was still attending Chantry High School and had not yet signed professional forms at Portman Road.

A tall and skilful striker, he was a key figure in the 1991/92 promotion team. missing only one league game and netting eleven league goals. Capped by England at U21 level, Jason stayed with Ipswich until August 1993 when he moved to Tottenham Hotspur for a then record fee, reported to be in the region of £1.9 million.

After four years at White Hart Lane, he made a brief return to Ipswich in 1997 before joining Northampton Town. He then joined Colchester United, eventually taking his overall league appearances beyond the 500 mark before persistent injuries forced him to quit the game. Incredibly, Jason's son Andre would later play for Town and also score on his debut while still only 16.

DAVID LINIGHAN

PLAYER PROFILE

DATE OF BIRTH:	**9 January 1965**
PLACE OF BIRTH:	**Hartlepool**
IPSWICH TOWN (ALL COMPS):	**328 Appearances · 13 Goals**
1991/92 (LEAGUE ONLY):	**36 Appearances · 3 Goals**

Having begun his career with hometown club Hartlepool United, David Linighan joined Ipswich Town in a £300,000 transfer from Shrewsbury Town in March 1988.

Linighan's move to Ipswich certainly created some serious family rivalry as his arrival at Portman Road coincided with his older brother Andy also plying his trade in East Anglian, with fierce rivals Norwich City.

A powerful, reliable and committed central-defender, Linighan made over 300 first-team appearances for the Blues during a highly successful seven-year spell in Suffolk.

He was voted the club's Player of the Season in 1990/91 and was once again a colossal presence at the heart of the Town defence during the 1991/92 title-winning campaign, where his performances saw him voted into the PFA Second Division Team of the Season.

Linighan netted three leagues goals in 1991/92 and was on target in back-to-back Second Division victories as Town won 2-1 at Wolves on November 23 before registering a comprehensive 4-0 Portman Road triumph over Tranmere Rovers seven days later.

After leaving Ipswich in 1995, Linighan played league football for Blackpool and Mansfield Town before drifting onto the non-league scene.

Town started September sitting proudly at the top of the league with ten points from four games, but in their next game, at home to Swindon Town, they were given a sharp reminder that their road to promotion glory still had a long way to go.

Inspired by player-manager Glenn Hoddle, the visitors completely outplayed Town for long periods to record an emphatic 4-1 victory. After falling behind to an early goal from White, Ipswich soon bounced back with an equaliser when Kiwomya capitalised on a poor goal-kick from Fraser Digby. For the remainder of the half it was a fairly even game, but after the visitors regained the lead through Calderwood just before the break, they took control, eventually scoring twice in the last ten minutes through Taylor and Hazard.

The following day, supporters were dealt another blow when the news broke that Town were about to sell central-defender Brian Gayle to Sheffield United for £800,000. The transfer gave the club a much needed injection of funds, but many supporters viewed the sale as a negative move. For Town's next game, at home to Southend United, John Lyall brought in Tony Humes to fill the number five shirt vacated by Gayle.

The game turned out to be a closely-fought encounter that was settled by a penalty just after the break when Southend 'keeper Sansome brought down Johnson for Thompson to step up and drive home the resulting spot-kick.

After the Swindon result, it was a welcome victory for John Lyall's team, but the following week they travelled up to Yorkshire to meet Barnsley where they suffered their first away defeat of the season. The game was played out in blustery conditions with the only goal coming in the 80th minute when Currie capitalised on poor defending by Town to clinch the points for the home side.

Town headed even further north for their next game, a difficult challenge against the much-fancied Newcastle United at St James' Park. Despite their indifferent form, Lyall named an unchanged side, but his plans were quickly thrown into disarray when Humes sustained a broken arm within minutes of the start. Yallop came off the bench to play alongside Linighan in a game that produced some great attacking football from both sides.

Town took the lead on 36 minutes when a great ball from Dozzell sent Kiwomya clear to fire home. The Ipswich striker had the ball in the net a few minutes later only for the effort to be disallowed for an infringement. The home side finally grabbed an equaliser after the break when Quinn fired home from the spot after Zondervan was adjudged to have brought down Brock inside the box.

RUMBELOWS' CUP ACTION AT DERBY COUNTY

John Lyall was now concentrating on finding a central-defender to plug the gap in the heart of Town's defence, and amazingly he turned his attention to Portman Road legend John Wark who had been training with the club since his release by Middlesbrough at the end of the previous season.

Yallop remained in the side when Town returned to home soil to face Bristol City in a hugely entertaining encounter. Allison gave the visitors an early lead, but Town were deservedly level before the break when Thompson fired home a terrific 20-yard free-kick. City were in front again on 56 minutes when Smith curled home a free-kick, but a few minutes later Town had a great opportunity to equalise when they were awarded a penalty after Kiwomya had been brought down in the box, only for Thompson to see his spot kick well saved by Welch. The home side weren't to be denied however and just after the hour mark, Linighan levelled the score. Town were now in total control, and after producing some of their best football of the season they were rewarded with two goals in quick succession from Kiwomya and Goddard to make the game safe.

A break from league action followed with an away fixture against Derby County in the second round of the Rumbelows Cup and a resolute display saw them deservedly earn a replay after a goalless draw. Having signed non-contractual forms, John Wark was named as substitute for the first time and would soon become a significant figure in the season ahead. He was on the bench again in Town's next game when goals from Johnson and Lowe secured maximum points with a 2-1 victory over Grimsby Town at Blundell Park.

DIVISION TWO

30 SEPTEMBER 1991	P	W	D	L	F	A	GD	P
1 Middlesbrough	11	8	1	2	18	8	10	25
2 **Ipswich Town**	**10**	**6**	**2**	**2**	**18**	**15**	**3**	**20**
3 Cambridge United	9	6	1	2	19	13	6	19
4 Swindon Town	9	5	2	2	21	13	8	17
5 Wolverhampton Wanderers	9	5	2	2	16	11	5	17
6 Leicester City	9	5	1	3	13	13	0	16
7 Portsmouth	9	4	3	2	9	7	2	15
8 Tranmere Rovers	9	3	5	1	15	12	3	14
9 Charlton Athletic	9	4	2	3	13	12	1	14
10 Southend United	9	4	2	3	9	8	1	14
11 Grimsby Town	9	4	2	3	16	16	0	14
12 Brighton and Hove Albion	10	4	2	4	15	15	0	14
13 Derby County	10	3	4	3	12	11	1	13
14 Bristol City	10	3	4	3	13	15	-2	13
15 Blackburn Rovers	9	3	3	3	7	8	-1	12
16 Millwall	9	3	2	4	16	14	2	11
17 Sunderland	10	3	2	5	17	17	0	11
18 Watford	9	3	1	5	11	13	-2	10
19 Port Vale	11	2	4	5	9	13	-4	10
20 Plymouth Argyle	9	2	2	5	12	17	-5	8
21 Barnsley	11	2	2	7	9	19	-10	8
22 Oxford United	9	2	1	6	12	17	-5	7
23 Newcastle United	10	1	4	5	14	20	-6	7
24 Bristol Rovers	9	1	2	6	11	18	-7	5

FRANK YALLOP

PLAYER PROFILE

DATE OF BIRTH:	**4 April 1964**
PLACE OF BIRTH:	**Watford**
IPSWICH TOWN (ALL COMPS):	**385 Appearances · 8 Goals**
1991/92 (LEAGUE ONLY):	**17 Appearances**

Frank Yallop grave great service to Ipswich Town and appeared in first-team fixtures across 13 consecutive seasons from 1983/84 to 1995/96.

Despite being born in Watford, the right-back enjoyed a successful international career with Canada for whom he was capped on 52 occasions - 38 of them as a Town player.

Handed his Ipswich debut as teenager in a First Division match away to Everton in March 1984, Yallop went on to serve under the management of Bobby Ferguson, John Duncan, John Lyall and George Burley.

The 1991/92 campaign saw him make 17 league appearances and his vast experience was a useful tool in helping the younger members of the side cope with the pressures of a promotion push.

Finishing his playing day in the USA with Tampa Bay Rowdies, Yallop went on to carve out a lengthy coaching and management career in the US as well as a having a couple of years in charge of the Canadian national team.

One of the clubs he managed in the US was Phoenix Rising - an appointment that links Yallop to the club's current American owners and his own long-held Portman Road roots.

EDWARD YOUDS

PLAYER PROFILE

DATE OF BIRTH:	**3 May 1970**
PLACE OF BIRTH:	**Liverpool**
IPSWICH TOWN (ALL COMPS):	**59 Appearances · 1 Goal**
1991/92 (LEAGUE ONLY):	**1 Appearance**

Scouser Eddie Youds started out at Everton and broke through to the Toffees' first team before joining Ipswich Town in 1991 for a fee of £250,000.

The central-defender, who had also played a handful of games during loan spells with Cardiff City and Wrexham, made his Town debut on 16 November 1991 as Town suffered a 1-0 defeat to Derby County at the Baseball Ground.

Replacing Frank Yallop in the 1-0 defeat against the Rams on his debut was Youds' only first-team outing in the 1991/92 title-winning campaign. However, he swiftly displayed the form that had earned him a glowing reputation as a youngster at Goodison Park as he went on to feature regularly for Town in the Premier League.

After 59 first-team appearances for Ipswich, Youds joined Bradford City on loan before completing a permanent move to Valley Parade. He captained the Bantams to Second Division play-off glory in 1996 and enjoyed another successful play-off campaign featuring for Charlton in their memorable penalty-shootout triumph over Sunderland in 1998 following an incredible 4-4 draw at Wembley.

GLENN PENNYFATHER

PLAYER PROFILE

DATE OF BIRTH:	**11 February 1963**
PLACE OF BIRTH:	**Billericay**
IPSWICH TOWN (ALL COMPS):	**19 Appearances · 1 Goal**
1991/92 (LEAGUE ONLY):	**3 Appearances**

A versatile performer who was equally at home in defence or in a midfield role, Glenn Pennyfather joined Ipswich Town in October 1989 following an £80,000 transfer from Crystal Palace.

Born in Billericay in 1963, Pennyfather began his career with nearby Southend United and gained cult status at Roots Hall after almost 250 league outings for the Essex club. He left the Shrimpers for Selhurst Park in 1987 and after two years moved to Portman Road.

Never a regular first-team starter, Pennyfather made three appearances in Town's 1991/92 promotion-winning team and was rewarded with a taste of Premier League action the following season. His final game for Town was a top-flight fixture against Sheffield Wednesday in March 1993. Following a loan spell at Bristol

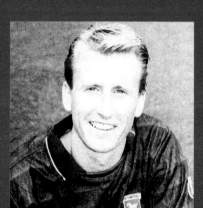

City, he completed a permanent switch to Ashton Gate as Town recuperated the initial £80,000 they paid for him.

Pennyfather later played non-league football for Stevenage Borough and Canvey Island before coaching and managing at Chelmsford City.

October began with a 3-1 victory over Bristol Rovers in the Zenith Data Systems Cup before they again returned to league action with a home fixture against Oxford United. The first half saw Town produce some brilliant attacking play with goals from Milton and Whitton giving them a 2-0 interval lead. After the break however, Lyall's men appeared to relax and after the visitors scored with ten minutes remaining there were some anxious moments for home fans as their team just about managed to hang on and secure an important win.

The following Tuesday saw Town entertain Derby County in the Rumbelows Cup replay and an early penalty gave them a great chance to grab the lead only for Thompson's kick to strike Peter Shilton's trailing leg and fly over the bar. Thereafter, the visitors took control and eventually ran out as comfortable winners with goals from Gee and Williams who netted from the spot.

Jason Dozzell had been missing for the Oxford United and Derby County games due to injury, but returned to the starting line-up for Town's next fixture at Brighton and Hove Albion. Milton gave Town a great start when he opened the scoring on 15 minutes, but they soon suffered a blow when Kiwomya limped off midway through the half to be replaced by Gregory.

Town held the lead until half-time, but their defence was finally breached shortly after the break when Byrne grabbed the equaliser. Soon afterwards however, Lyall's men were in front again when Dozzell netted his 50th senior goal, but the lead was short-lived when Chivers headed home to earn Albion a share of the spoils. The draw kept Town in touch with early pace-setters Middlesbrough who were sitting top of the table, but also began a sequence of eight consecutive league games without a win that saw them slip from second spot to ninth place in Division Two.

After a disappointing goalless draw with Millwall at Portman Road, Town returned to cup action with another home fixture, against First Division Luton Town in the Zenith Data Systems Cup. A late goal from Telfer appeared to have secured the Hatters a place in the next round, but a last gasp equaliser by Lowe sent the game into extra time. With neither side able to conjure up the winning goal the tie went to a penalty shoot-out with Town finally triumphing with Craig Forrest emerging as the hero saving two of the Luton's spot kicks.

Town's next game was away to Portsmouth, but before that, John Lyall made a rare foray into the transfer market by signing John Moncur on a month's loan from Tottenham Hotspur with a view to a permanent signing. The new man was immediately named as substitute for the Fratton Park game and soon found himself in the thick of the action when he entered the fray to replace Lowe who had suffered a severe head injury early in the game.

19

JOHN WARK V MILLWALL AT PORTMAN ROAD

JASON DOZZELL SCORES AT BRIGHTON

...AND GOES CLOSE AGAINST MILLWALL

Soon afterwards, great work by Zondervan and Stockwell set up Milton to give Town a well-deserved lead, but after Burns had netted the equaliser, they had to rely on some brilliant goalkeeping by Forrest to earn them a point.

October drew to a close with a visit to Charlton Athletic who at the time were playing their home games at West Ham United's Upton Park after temporarily losing the use of The Valley. John Lyall introduced Darren Edmonds, a new signing who had moved from Leeds United to Portman Road on a free transfer. The new man watched from the bench as his new teammates came from behind to earn another away point, Whitton grabbing the equaliser after Gatting had headed the home side in front.

DIVISION TWO

	31 OCTOBER 1991	P	W	D	L	F	A	GD	P
1	Middlesbrough	15	9	2	4	20	11	9	29
2	Cambridge United	13	9	1	3	26	16	10	28
3	Charlton Athletic	15	8	4	3	22	15	7	28
4	**Ipswich Town**	**15**	**7**	**6**	**2**	**24**	**20**	**4**	**27**
5	Swindon Town	13	8	2	3	30	16	14	26
6	Derby County	14	7	4	3	22	14	8	25
7	Leicester City	14	8	1	5	20	19	1	25
8	Blackburn Rovers	13	6	3	4	18	14	4	21
9	Bristol City	14	5	5	4	18	21	-3	20
10	Wolverhampton Wanderers	13	5	4	4	18	17	1	19
11	Southend United	14	5	4	5	17	17	0	19
12	Portsmouth	13	5	4	4	13	13	0	19
13	Millwall	14	5	3	6	23	21	2	18
14	Grimsby Town	13	5	2	6	19	22	-3	17
15	Port Vale	15	4	5	6	15	18	-3	17
16	Tranmere Rovers	13	3	7	3	18	17	1	16
17	Sunderland	14	4	4	6	25	26	-1	16
18	Watford	14	5	1	8	15	18	-3	16
19	Brighton and Hove Albion	15	4	3	8	20	27	-7	15
20	Newcastle United	14	3	5	6	22	27	-5	14
21	Barnsley	15	4	2	9	15	24	-9	14
22	Oxford United	15	4	1	10	22	29	-7	13
23	Bristol Rovers	13	2	4	7	14	21	-7	10
24	Plymouth Argyle	13	2	3	8	14	27	-13	9

Next up came Town's third consecutive away game, a tough challenge against Leicester City at Filbert Street, and again they emerged with a well-earned point following a terrific game that was widely regarded as a credit to the Second Division.

Town had to defend in depth throughout the first period with Forrest regularly denying the home forwards with a series of superb saves.

21

PAUL GODDARD

PLAYER PROFILE

DATE OF BIRTH:	**12 October 1959**
PLACE OF BIRTH:	**Harlington, Middlesex**
IPSWICH TOWN (ALL COMPS):	**83 Appearances · 13 Goals**
1991/92 (LEAGUE ONLY):	**24 Appearances · 4 Goals**

Born in Harlington in Middlesex, Paul Goddard signed for Queens Park Rangers as a youth player in 1977 quickly earning a reputation as a goalscorer of real potential.

After progressing through the ranks, he was soon hitting the target on a regular basis at first-team level which quickly attracted the attention of a number of top clubs including West Ham United who at the time were managed by none other than a certain John Lyall.

In 1980, it was indeed West Ham United who clinched his signature with a bid of £800,000. Paul enjoyed a great career at Upton Park netting 71 goals during his six years at the club and his goalscoring prowess earned him a full England cap when he made a scoring international debut against Iceland in Reykjavik in June 1982.

Four years later, Paul joined Newcastle United before having spells with Derby County and Millwall. Then in 1991, he teamed up with John Lyall again, signing for Ipswich town on a free transfer. After Town's promotion in 1992, Paul enjoyed a few more years playing Premiership football before retiring from the game in 1994. Soon afterwards Paul took over as Ipswich Town's youth team coach.

PAUL GODDARD 1993/94

CRAIG FORREST 1993/94

CRAIG FORREST

An outstanding goalkeeper and a great servant to Ipswich Town, Craig Forrest was spotted by Town scouts in 1984 while playing in local football in British Columbia.

While still only 17 years of age, Craig arrived at Portman Road as an apprentice and quickly progressed through the ranks and, after a loan spell with Colchester United during the 1987/88 season, he made his first-team debut for Town to begin a career that would eventually span nine seasons.

He was an ever-present during the 1991/92 championship-winning season and in 1994/95 he was voted Ipswich Town Player of the Year.

During his time at Portman Road he played for Canada in the 1987 U20 World Cup before eventually winning 56 full international caps for his country. In both 1994 and 2000 Craig was voted Canadian International Player of the Year and was inducted into the Canadian Soccer Hall of Fame in 2007.

Craig's Ipswich Town career came to an end in 1997 when he joined West Ham United in a £500,000 transfer where he spent five seasons before retiring from the game in 2002. He now occupies the post of Canadian FIFA Ambassador for SOS Children's Villages.

Shortly after the break, the deadlock was broken when Wark lent his weight to the attack by heading home a corner from Thompson, but within ten minutes the home side regained the initiative with goals from Kitson and Oldfield.

Town were not to be denied however, and with 14 minutes remaining Johnson headed home Yallop's cross to earn Lyall's team the point their enterprising play thoroughly deserved.

Hopes were high for a return to winning ways with consecutive home games against Sunderland and Cambridge United, but defeats in both of these games saw Town slip badly in the promotion race dropping to seventh place. Sunderland were far the better side and would have won more convincingly had they converted the numerous chances that came their way. Instead, they had to rely on a solitary headed goal scored by Armstrong following great work by John Byrne, a new signing from Brighton and Hove Albion.

Despite the disappointment of the Sunderland result, a crowd of over 20,000 packed into Portman Road four days later for the visit of local rivals Cambridge United for a game that saw John Wark make his 500th appearance for the club. Town started the game well with Milton and Dozzell both hitting the woodwork early on, but an injury to Whitton disrupted their plans and Cambridge began to take control. Just before the break, Rowett headed the visitors in front from a corner after which Town struggled to get back into the game.

Nevertheless, with only eleven minutes remaining, they looked to have snatched an unlikely point when Stockwell ran onto a great pass from Johnson to fire home. Their joy was short-lived however, and in the dying minutes Claridge netted a somewhat fortuitous winner for the visitors, his shot deflecting off Linighan giving Forrest no chance.

The recent run of poor results no doubt prompted John Lyall to again move into the transfer market, this time to stabilise Town's defence with the signing of Eddie Youds, a £250,000 capture from Everton. Youds was immediately brought into the team for Town's next fixture away to Derby County, but his Ipswich career could hardly have got off to a worse start when he left the field on the hour mark with what would turn out to be a serious knee injury. Ironically, it was while Town's new signing was receiving treatment on the touchline that the Rams netted the only goal of the game and consign John Lyall's team to their third consecutive defeat.

JOHNSON
RESCUES A POINT

Now ninth in Division Two, Town were desperate for a positive result in their next game, against Wolves at Molineux. Things certainly did not start well when the home side took the lead through Birch after only seven minutes and throughout the first period only desperate defending prevented Wanderers from adding to their advantage.

It was a much improved Town performance after the break and the game swung their way in a stunning six-minute spell with goals from Linighan and a great solo effort from Dozzell that would turn out to be the winner and secure their first win in over six weeks.

Town's next game saw them return to cup action when two goals from Chris Kiwomya earned a credible 2-2 draw against Chelsea at Stamford Bridge in the Zenith Data Systems Cup only for them to finally lose 4-3 in a penalty shoot-out. However, the following Saturday, they bounced back in style with a terrific performance to record a 4-0 victory over Tranmere Rovers, their biggest win of the season so far. Goals from Milton and Thompson gave Town a first-half lead with Linighan heading home a third mid-way through the second period before Wark rifled home a penalty in the final minute.

DIVISION TWO

	30 NOVEMBER 1991	P	W	D	L	F	A	GD	P
1	Cambridge United	19	11	5	3	32	20	12	38
2	Middlesbrough	21	11	4	6	29	18	11	37
3	Derby County	20	10	4	6	30	22	8	34
4	Blackburn Rovers	19	10	4	5	26	18	8	34
5	**Ipswich Town**	21	9	7	5	33	27	6	34
6	Leicester City	20	10	3	7	26	25	1	33
7	Swindon Town	19	9	5	5	37	24	13	32
8	Southend United	20	9	5	6	30	25	5	32
9	Charlton Athletic	21	9	5	7	25	22	3	32
10	Portsmouth	19	9	5	5	22	19	3	32
11	Bristol City	20	7	7	6	23	27	-4	28
12	Port Vale	21	7	6	8	22	25	-3	27
13	Millwall	20	7	5	8	30	27	3	26
14	Tranmere Rovers	18	6	8	4	22	22	0	26
15	Sunderland	20	6	5	9	31	32	-1	23
16	Watford	20	7	2	11	22	26	-4	23
17	Newcastle United	21	5	8	8	30	36	-6	23
18	Brighton and Hove Albion	21	6	5	10	26	32	-6	23
19	Barnsley	21	7	2	12	22	31	-9	23
20	Wolverhampton Wanderers	20	6	4	10	26	30	-4	22
21	Bristol Rovers	20	5	7	8	26	31	-5	22
22	Grimsby Town	19	6	4	9	23	31	-8	22
23	Oxford United	21	5	3	13	28	37	-9	18
24	Plymouth Argyle	19	5	3	11	17	31	-14	18

GAVIN JOHNSON

PLAYER PROFILE

DATE OF BIRTH:	**10 October 1970**
PLACE OF BIRTH:	**Stowmarket**
IPSWICH TOWN (ALL COMPS):	**160 Appearances · 16 Goals**
1991/92 (LEAGUE ONLY):	**42 Appearances · 5 Goals**

Stowmarket-born Gavin Johnson worked his way through the youth and reserve ranks at Portman Road before going on to play a major role in Town's 1991/92 promotion-winning campaign.

Johnson made his first-team debut in February 1989 as the Blues defeated Barnsley 2-0 at Portman Road. He found regular first-team football hard to come by over the following two seasons, but really made the Blues' left-back berth his own in 1991/92.

As Ipswich stormed up the Second Division table en route to title success and promotion glory, Johnson chipped in five goals as he enhanced his growing reputation as an attacking full-back. Among his five-goal haul was the strike that sealed both promotion and the title as Town drew 1-1 away to Oxford United on 25 April 1992.

After starring in the 1991/92 triumph, Johnson then took the mantle of scoring the club's first-ever Premier League goal as the Blues played out a 1-1 opening-day draw against Aston Villa at Portman Road.

Johnson made a total of 160 appearances for Town before going to enjoy further promotion success with Wigan Athletic in 1996/97 and Northampton Town in 2005/06.

JOHNSON
TOWN'S FIRST PREMIER LEAGUE GOALSCORER

DAVID LOWE

PLAYER PROFILE

DATE OF BIRTH:	**30 August 1965**
PLACE OF BIRTH:	**Liverpool**
IPSWICH TOWN (ALL COMPS):	**159 Appearances · 44 Goals**
1991/92 (LEAGUE ONLY):	**14 Appearances · 1 Goal**

An attack-minded midfielder, who tended to operate on the right, David Lowe joined Ipswich Town in the summer of 1987 from Wigan Athletic.

Lowe had played under former Portman Road favourite Bryan Hamilton during his time at Springfield Park and was one of the first Town signings under management of the John Duncan.

In his debut season at Portman Road he topped the club's 1987/88 scoring charts with 18 goals and his club form won him two caps at U21 level for England.

Lowe's Town career saw him make 159 appearances and fire home an impressive 44 goals for the club. The 1991/92 season proved to be his last at Portman Road and his final league goal helped secure a vital early season triumph away to Grimsby Town in September 1991.

With first-team opportunities proving less frequent, Lowe joined Second Division rivals Port Vale on loan for the remainder of the season - swapping Town's promotion push for a relegation battle in the Potteries.

Following Ipswich Town's promotion to the newly-formed Premier League, and Vale's relegation, Lowe remained in the second tier for 1992/93 when he completed a £200,000 move to Leicester City.

Predictably, John Lyall named an unchanged side for Town's next fixture, a long trip to the south west to meet struggling Plymouth Argyle, but they were unable to reproduce the form they had shown in the Tranmere game. After falling behind in the 26th minute, the game quickly became an uphill battle that was made infinitely more difficult when Whitton was shown a red card early in the second half. Despite coming more into the game in the closing stages, Town were unable to unlock a resolute Argyle defence as the home side hung on to secure the victory.

With winter conditions now beginning to play havoc with football fixtures throughout the country, Town's next game at home to Watford was postponed due to the state of the ice-covered Portman Road pitch. A week later they did manage to return to action against Swindon at the County Ground when only an inspired display by home 'keeper Nicky Hammond denied Town the victory their performance deserved, but instead, they had to settle for a point from a goalless draw.

Next up, Town supporters were served up some real Christmas fayre with two massive home games. The first against Charlton Athletic on Boxing Day saw Glenn Pennyfather make his first appearance for the first-team since March 1990 as he was brought in to replace Whitton who was suspended following his dismissal at Plymouth. Pennyfather was actually involved in Town's opening goal when he set up Kiwomya with an easy chance which he drove into the net from close-range. Kiwomya was on target again just after the break when he was sent clear by Milton to slide the ball past Bolder in the Charlton goal. After that, the visitors were never really in the contest and to round off a thoroughly bad day, Webster was sent-off in the closing minutes for a second bookable offence.

Two days later, a crowd of 17,657 turned up to see whether Town could overcome Blackburn Rovers, the league's big spenders whose side included the likes of Mike Newell and David Speedie. The game turned out to be a thrilling encounter that saw Rovers take an early lead, although only a brilliant save from Mimms prevented Dozzell levelling the scores just before the break.

The home side were not to be denied however and just two minutes into the second half, Johnson grabbed the equaliser with a brilliant diving header from a great cross by Whitton. Thereafter the game developed into a real end-to-end battle with Town supporters getting behind their team in great style as they pushed forward looking for the winner.

As the game entered the closing stages either side might have scored, but with just five minutes remaining Dozzell produced a stunning strike to win the day, turning brilliantly to fire home after some great build-up play involving Thompson, Whitton and Kiwomya. The result saw Town move up to third place in Division Two and bring the curtain down on 1991 in great fashion.

DIVISION TWO

31 DECEMBER 1991		P	W	D	L	F	A	GD	P
1	Blackburn Rovers	23	12	5	6	33	21	12	41
2	Cambridge United	23	11	8	4	36	25	11	41
3	**Ipswich Town**	**25**	**11**	**8**	**6**	**37**	**29**	**8**	**41**
4	Middlesbrough	24	12	5	7	32	24	8	41
5	Southend United	25	11	7	7	35	30	5	40
6	Leicester City	24	12	4	8	31	28	3	40
7	Portsmouth	23	11	6	6	29	21	8	39
8	Derby County	23	11	5	7	33	25	8	38
9	Swindon Town	23	9	9	5	41	28	13	36
10	Charlton Athletic	24	10	6	8	28	26	2	36
11	Millwall	24	9	6	9	37	36	1	33
12	Bristol City	24	8	8	8	30	34	-4	32
13	Tranmere Rovers	21	7	10	4	25	24	1	31
14	Port Vale	26	7	10	9	26	32	-6	31
15	Watford	24	9	3	12	29	29	0	30
16	Wolverhampton Wanderers	24	8	6	10	30	31	-1	30
17	Barnsley	26	8	6	12	29	35	-6	30
18	Sunderland	25	8	5	12	33	37	-4	29
19	Newcastle United	26	6	10	10	36	44	-8	28
20	Grimsby Town	23	7	6	10	28	37	-9	27
21	Bristol Rovers	25	6	8	11	32	42	-10	26
22	Plymouth Argyle	23	7	4	12	22	34	-12	25
23	Brighton and Hove Albion	26	6	6	14	33	44	-11	24
24	Oxford United	24	6	3	15	32	41	-9	21

John Lyall's team kicked off the New Year with a trip to the Potteries to face Port Vale and were no doubt keen to eradicate the memories of a 5-0 defeat at Vale Park two years earlier. Town started the game very much in the driving seat and after Linighan and Johnson had gone close, Kiwomya gave them a deserved lead just before the break.

Sent clear by Whitton, the Town striker kept his cool and rounded the Vale 'keeper to calmly slot the ball into the empty net. Eight minutes into the second half he was on target again when he doubled their advantage, scoring from close-range after Linighan had headed Thompson's corner into his path. Soon afterwards however, a great 25-yard strike from Hughes brought the home side back into the game and only a brilliant save by Forrest just before the end helped preserve Town's lead and secure another great victory.

Now sitting in second place in Division Two, Town were now able to turn their attention to the FA Cup third round with the visit of Division Three Hartlepool to Portman Road. Despite the bookies emphatically favouring a home win, a real upset looked to be on the cards after Baker put the visitors in front just before the break and only a late goal by Dozzell saved the day to earn Town a replay.

CHRIS KIWOMYA

PLAYER PROFILE

DATE OF BIRTH:	**2 December 1969**
PLACE OF BIRTH:	**Huddersfield**
IPSWICH TOWN (ALL COMPS):	**260 Appearances · 64 Goals**
1991/92 (LEAGUE ONLY):	**43 Appearances · 16 Goals**

Livewire striker Chris Kiwomya was Town's 16-goal leading league scorer in the club's 1991/92 Second Division title-winning campaign.

A product of the club's youth set-up, Kiwomya made his professional debut in a 1-1 Portman Road draw with Bradford City in September 1988 and went on to enjoy a 64-goal Town career.

Forming an almost telepathic on-pitch relationship with Jason Dozzell, Kiwomya's contribution to the 1991/92 success was certainly one of his most productive campaigns for the Blues.

Blessed with great pace and intelligent movement, Kiwomya was on target in the opening home game of 1991/92 as Town edged past Port Vale 2-1. He also fired a brace in the return fixture as Ipswich triumphed 2-1 at Vale Park on New Year's Day 1992, with that double coming on the back of him scoring both goals in the 2-0 Boxing Day win at home to Charlton. Another two in the 5-2 win over Portsmouth in February were followed by his final league double of a prolific campaign at home to Barnsley in March as John Lyall's men closed in on promotion.

Having made over 250 appearances, Kiwomya left Town in January 1995 in a £1.5M move to Arsenal. After retiring, his coaching career took him back to Town where he oversaw the reserve team and U18s. In 2013, he had a brief spell managing Notts County.

ROMEO ZONDERVAN

PLAYER PROFILE

DATE OF BIRTH:	**4 March 1959**
PLACE OF BIRTH:	**Paramaribo, Suriname**
IPSWICH TOWN (ALL COMPS):	**325 Appearances · 20 Goals**
1991/92 (LEAGUE ONLY):	**28 Appearances**

The versatility displayed by Dutchman Romeo Zondervan saw him make 325 appearances in a Town shirt. Primarily a midfielder, Zondervan's flexibility made him something of a manager's dream as he could slip into the side in virtually any position and do a job for the team.

He began his career in Holland with ADO Den Haag and FC Twente. After gaining international recognition with the Netherlands in 1981, he moved to England in 1982 when he linked up with his former Twente teammate, and future Tottenham manager, Martin Jol at West Bromwich Albion.

After two years at the Hawthorns, Zondervan arrived at Portman Road in a £70,000 switch in March 1984. He made an instant impression at Portman Road and landed the Player of the Season accolade in 1986/87, before captaining the side in 1988/89 and 1999/90.

The 1991/92 season proved to be his last at the club and what a fitting end to his Ipswich career as the club returned to the top flight as Second Division champions. After making 28 league appearances in his final season in Suffolk, Zondervan opted to return to the Netherlands when he joined NAC Breda.

Before that, Lyall's team faced another challenge in the north east, this time to face promotion rivals Middlesbrough in a vital league game. Pennyfather was back in the side replacing the injured Thompson who missed his first game of the season. There was little action to speak of in the first half, but after the break, the home side took control with Town's rearguard struggling to keep them at bay and it came as no surprise when Payton scrambled home the winner.

Still in the north east, a few days later, the Town party made the short journey to Hartlepool for the FA Cup third round replay and this time they made no mistake with a solid performance with goals from Dozzell and Milton securing a 2-0 victory and a home tie against Bournemouth in the fourth round.

The following Saturday, in their 2,000th Football League match, Town rounded off their January programme with a well-deserved 1-0 victory over Bristol Rovers at Portman Road. They were in control from the start and only the woodwork and some inspired keeping by Parkin in the Rovers goal kept them at bay in a one-sided first half. The breakthrough came midway through the second period when Milton latched onto a loose ball in the crowded goalmouth to fire past the unsighted Rovers 'keeper and secure the points.

DIVISION TWO

	31 JANUARY 1992	P	W	D	L	F	A	GD	P
1	Blackburn Rovers	26	14	6	6	41	24	17	48
2	Southend United	28	13	8	7	42	32	10	47
3	**Ipswich Town**	**28**	**13**	**8**	**7**	**40**	**31**	**9**	**47**
4	Cambridge United	27	12	9	6	39	28	11	45
5	Middlesbrough	27	13	6	8	34	27	7	45
6	Leicester City	27	13	6	8	37	32	5	45
7	Portsmouth	27	12	7	8	35	27	8	43
8	Swindon Town	27	11	9	7	47	35	12	42
9	Charlton Athletic	27	11	7	9	34	33	1	40
10	Wolverhampton Wanderers	27	11	6	10	37	31	6	39
11	Derby County	26	11	6	9	35	29	6	39
12	Sunderland	28	11	5	12	43	40	3	38
13	Millwall	27	10	6	11	42	45	-3	36
14	Tranmere Rovers	26	7	14	5	27	27	0	35
15	Bristol City	27	8	10	9	32	40	-8	34
16	Watford	28	9	6	13	32	35	-3	33
17	Bristol Rovers	29	8	9	12	35	44	-9	33
18	Grimsby Town	26	9	6	11	30	39	-9	33
19	Plymouth Argyle	26	9	5	12	30	39	-9	32
20	Port Vale	29	7	11	11	29	38	-9	32
21	Barnsley	29	8	6	15	31	43	-12	30
22	Brighton and Hove Albion	29	7	8	14	37	46	-9	29
23	Newcastle United	29	6	11	12	41	54	-13	29
24	Oxford United	28	6	5	17	37	48	-11	23

GOALMOUTH ACTION FROM THE FA CUP THIRD ROUND TIE WITH HARTLEPOOL WHICH FINISHED 1-1 AT PORTMAN ROAD

33

PHILIP WHELAN

PLAYER PROFILE

DATE OF BIRTH:	**7 August 1972**
PLACE OF BIRTH:	**Stockport**
IPSWICH TOWN (ALL COMPS):	**92 Appearances · 2 Goals**
1991/92 (LEAGUE ONLY):	**8 Appearances · 2 Goals**

Defender Phil Whelan's burst onto the first-team scene at Portman Road coincided with the club's final push for promotion in April 1992.

The Stockport-born centre-back agreed professional terms with Town in the summer of 1990, but spent the majority of the 1991/92 seasons in the reserve team. His first-team debut came in October 1991 when he played in a Full Members Cup match away to Bristol Rovers.

Whelan's long wait for a league debut finally arrived on 4 April 1992 as Town travelled to Southend United. He commemorated the occasion in style, joining teammate Neil Thompson on the scoresheet in a vital 2-1 win.

With a taste for games and goals, Whelan did it again three days later as he marked his Portman Road bow with a goal in the 2-1 victory over Wolverhampton Wanderers.

A first-team regular across then following two seasons, Whelan left Town at the end of the 1994/95 relegation season when he joined Middlesbrough. His playing career concluded with spells at Oxford United, Rotherham United and Southend United.

JOHN MONCUR

PLAYER PROFILE

DATE OF BIRTH:	**22 September 1966**
PLACE OF BIRTH:	**Stepney**
IPSWICH TOWN (ALL COMPS):	**6 Appearances**
1991/92 (LEAGUE ONLY):	**6 Appearances**

A cultured midfielder, who began his career at Tottenham Hotspur, John Moncur made six appearances for Town while on loan at Portman Road in 1991/92.

Comfortable on the ball, yet certainly not afraid of doing his bit to win possession, Stepney-born Moncur spent eight years on the books at White Hart Lane as he progressed through the ranks with the North London club.

During his early years as Spurs, Moncur gained valuable first-team experience with loan spells at Doncaster Rovers, Cambridge United, Portsmouth and Brentford before joining Town in 1991. Moncur was on familiar ground when he was handed an Ipswich debut by John Lyall against one of his former loan clubs - as he featured in a 1-1 draw away to Portsmouth in October 1991. His Town career comprised of five starts and one substitute appearance and he ended his Suffolk stay with a 2-1 victory over Wolves at Molineux before returning to Tottenham.

He was later signed by Spurs legend Glenn Hoddle for Swindon Town and helped the Wiltshire side reach the Premier League before enjoying a lengthy spell with West Ham United.

DAVID GREGORY

PLAYER PROFILE

DATE OF BIRTH:	**23 January 1970**
PLACE OF BIRTH:	**Polstead, Suffolk**
IPSWICH TOWN (ALL COMPS):	**43 Appearances · 6 Goals**
1991/92 (LEAGUE ONLY):	**1 Appearance**

A product of the Ipswich Town youth system, midfielder David Gregory spent ten years at Portman Road during which he enjoyed a loan spell with Hereford United before severing his ties with Town in 1995 to join Colchester United at Layer Road.

He is perhaps best remembered for scoring the winning goal from the penalty spot in the 1998 Play-Off final at Wembley and in April 2013, perhaps in recognition of his Wembley heroics, he was inducted into the Colchester United Hall of Fame.

DAVID GREGORY CHALLENGES WIMBLEDON'S VINNIE JONES WITH TEAMMATE SIMON MILTON, DECEMBER 1994

A crowd of over 26,000, Portman Road's biggest for almost ten years, were packed into the stadium for the visit of Liverpool, the bookies favourites to lift the FA Cup.

After seeing their FA Cup fourth round tie against Bournemouth postponed due to the state of the frozen Portman Road pitch, Town began February with an emphatic 3-2 victory over Millwall at The Den. However, the victory was much more clear-cut than the scoreline suggests. After dominating the early stages, Dozzell put the visitors ahead in the 33rd minute when he netted from close range after Kiwomya had set up the chance with a great cross.

Five minutes into the second half they doubled their advantage when Thompson hammered the ball into the net after Davison had failed to hold Dozzell's close-range effort. Midway through the half the game looked to be over when Kiwomya netted a third from a cross by Dozzell, but soon afterwards, John Wark was forced to leave the field with a hamstring injury which seemed to inspire something of a fight back from the home side. Rae quickly reduced the arrears then, with five minutes remaining, Linighan brought down Kerr in the box and the Millwall forward stepped up to convert the resulting penalty leaving Town to face a nervy few minutes before the final whistle.

Fortunately, John Wark was declared fit for Town's next game, the re-arranged FA Cup fourth round tie against Bournemouth which had now taken on added significance following the fifth-round draw that had presented the winners with a mouth-watering home tie against Liverpool. Having knocked out Newcastle United in the previous round, the Third Division side certainly could not be taken lightly, but again John Lyall's team produced a professional performance to record an emphatic 3-0 victory with goals from Dozzell, Whitton and Kiwomya.

The forthcoming tie against Liverpool certainly had supporters buzzing and no doubt dreaming of a trip to Wembley's twin towers. Certainly their team was beginning to show great form and the week before the Liverpool tie they produced probably their best performance of the season to hammer Portsmouth 5-2, a terrific attacking display that included a brace apiece for Dozzell and Kiwomya.

Next to arrive at Portman Road was the mighty Liverpool and the star-studded Merseysiders certainly looked an awesome proposition, but Town more than held their own in a game that was spoilt by a gale-force wind swirling around Portman Road. In fact, they were much the better side in the first half with Johnson and Kiwomya missing presentable opportunities and just before the break, Wark sent a thumping header against the Liverpool crossbar. That was the nearest either side came to breaking the deadlock in what developed into a dull goalless draw that provided little entertainment for spectators, and meant that Town had to travel up to Anfield for the replay ten days later.

Before that they were on Merseyside again, this time to face Tranmere Rovers in an important Division Two game that saw them clinch a hugely important victory with Simon Milton netting the only goal of the game mid-way through the second half.

The Liverpool replay attracted huge interest nationally with Sky Sports deciding to screen the match live. Again, John Lyall's team produced a brave performance and in the early stages they were much the better side, only to fall behind to a Ray Houghton goal just before the break.

However, throughout the second period, Town pressed forward continually looking for the equaliser that their adventurous play deserved and they were rewarded ten minutes from time when Johnson silenced the home fans after heading home Whitton's cross in great style to take the tie to extra-time.

Amazingly, the first period of extra-time saw Town take the lead when Grobbelaar failed to hold Dozzell's shot, allowing the Ipswich striker to follow up and drive the ball into the net. With a real upset looking to be on the cards Liverpool surged back into the game and after Molby had rifled home a superb 25-yard free-kick, McManaman put them in front with a brilliant individual effort.

After that there was no way back for Town, but they could take great credit for an outstanding performance against one of the best teams in the English game who would eventually go on to lift the FA Cup with a 2-0 victory over Sunderland at Wembley a few months later.

The following Saturday, it was back to league action again with an important home game against relegation-threatened Plymouth Argyle. Predictably, Town failed to reach the heights of the previous game at Anfield, but they did manage to secure a 2-0 victory to maintain their second-place standing in Division Two. After a dull first half, Town opened the scoring early in the second period, the goal coming after Argyle 'keeper Rhys Wilmot collided with his own defender Robbie Turner allowing Kiwomya to run on and place the loose ball into the empty net.

Unfortunately for Turner, the incident left him with a broken leg and after he was stretchered from the pitch, the visitors were forced to abandon their sweeper system. Thereafter, Town were much the better side, although there were only two minutes remaining when they managed to make the points safe with a second goal, a terrific diving header by Whitton from a great cross by Johnson.

SO CLOSE
AT ANFIELD

JOHNSON'S HEADER TAKES THE TIE INTO EXTRA-TIME

DOZZELL SCORES AGAINST THE REDS

SIMON MILTON

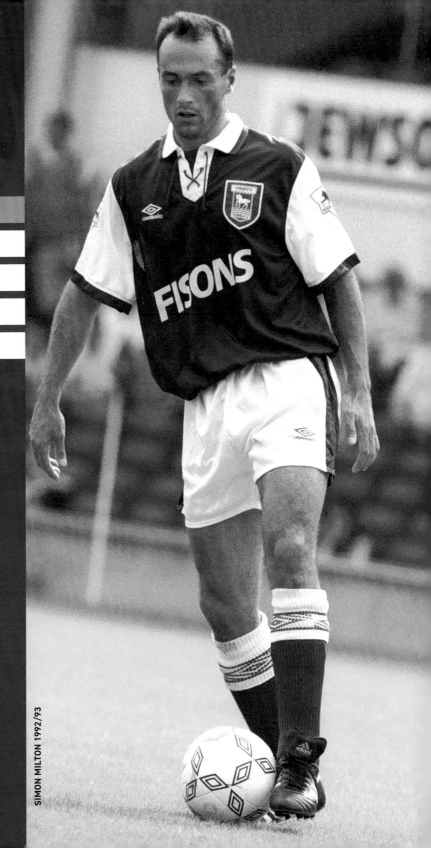

SIMON MILTON 1992/93

PLAYER PROFILE

DATE OF BIRTH:	**23 August 1963**
PLACE OF BIRTH:	**Fulham**
IPSWICH TOWN (ALL COMPS):	**332 Appearances · 54 Goals**
1991/92 (LEAGUE ONLY):	**34 Appearances · 7 Goals**

A member of the Ipswich Town FC Hall of Fame, midfielder Simon Milton was plucked from non-league football before going on to gain legendary status at Portman Road.

Although Milton's potential was initially spotted by Bobby Ferguson, John Duncan was the Town manager when the midfielder agreed a £5,000 switch from Bury Town. His Town debut arrived in a League Cup tie at home to Northampton Town in September 1987 and he gained some highly beneficial league experience with loan spells at both Exeter City and Torquay United.

Milton established himself as a first-team regular throughout the late 1980s and early '90s and gained popularity with a late winning goal in a Full Members Cup victory over Norwich City.

Certainly a key component in the 1991/92 title triumph, Milton netted seven league goals as Town secured a return to the top flight with the former Bury Town man scoring match-winners against Bristol Rovers and Tranmere Rovers.

Upon conclusion of a 330-game Town career in 1998, Milton became an Academy co-ordinator and a highly respected club ambassador.

JOHN WARK

PLAYER PROFILE	
DATE OF BIRTH:	**4 August 1957**
PLACE OF BIRTH:	**Glasgow**
IPSWICH TOWN (ALL COMPS):	**679 Appearances · 179 Goals**
1991/92 (LEAGUE ONLY):	**37 Appearances · 3 Goals**

Town legend John Wark enjoyed three spells as a player at Portman Road, with the attacking midfielder becoming the heartbeat of Bobby Robson's team that enjoyed great success in the late '70s and early '80s.

Born in Glasgow in 1957, Wark began his career at Town and debuted in the 1974/75 campaign as Ipswich finally defeated Leeds United in a FA Cup sixth round tie at the fourth time of asking. He went on to net a phenomenal 36 goals from midfield in Town's historic 1980/81 campaign and was voted the PFA Player of the Year as Ipswich competed for silverware on three fronts.

Wark's outstanding contribution to Town's bid for a league and FA Cup double ended with the club winning the UEFA Cup and finishing as runners-up to Aston Villa in the First Division title race, while their Wembley dream ended at the semi-final stage.

In March 1984, he joined First Division champions Liverpool before returning to Portman Road for his second spell in Suffolk in January 1988. As a free agent in the summer of 1990, Wark departed Ipswich for a second time when he signed for Middlesbrough.

The club's 1991/92 Second Division title-winning campaign coincided with the start of Wark's third and final spell at Ipswich. He made 37 appearances as Town topped the table and prepared for life in the Premier League.

41

DIVISION TWO

29 FEBRUARY 1992		P	W	D	L	F	A	GD	P
1	Blackburn Rovers	33	18	8	7	53	31	22	62
2	**Ipswich Town**	**32**	**17**	**8**	**7**	**51**	**35**	**16**	**59**
3	Cambridge United	33	16	10	7	49	31	18	58
4	Southend United	34	15	8	11	49	41	8	53
5	Middlesbrough	30	15	7	8	37	28	9	52
6	Derby County	32	15	6	11	42	35	7	51
7	Leicester City	32	15	6	11	42	39	3	51
8	Portsmouth	32	14	8	10	43	34	9	50
9	Swindon Town	32	13	10	9	52	39	13	49
10	Charlton Athletic	33	14	7	12	40	38	2	49
11	Millwall	33	13	7	13	52	52	0	46
12	Wolverhampton Wanderers	31	12	7	12	41	36	5	43
13	Sunderland	33	12	7	14	47	46	1	43
14	Barnsley	34	11	8	15	36	44	-8	41
15	Bristol Rovers	34	10	10	14	41	54	-13	40
16	Tranmere Rovers	30	8	15	7	32	34	-2	39
17	Grimsby Town	31	10	9	12	37	46	-9	39
18	Watford	32	10	7	15	34	39	-5	37
19	Newcastle United	34	8	12	14	49	63	-14	36
20	Bristol City	32	8	11	13	34	50	-16	35
21	Port Vale	34	7	13	14	32	44	-12	34
22	Plymouth Argyle	32	9	7	16	32	48	-16	34
23	Oxford United	33	9	6	18	47	54	-7	33
24	Brighton and Hove Albion	34	8	9	17	44	55	-11	33

February had proved to be a great month for Ipswich Town and it came as no surprise when John Lyall was named the Division Two Manager of the Month, the first time in ten years that any Town manager had won such an award.

March began with a 1-0 victory over Watford at Vicarage Road, although they were almost denied the points by an outstanding performance from the Hornets 'keeper David James. The only goal of the game came four minutes from time when Whitton fired home following great work by Kiwomya and Thompson.

A clash with promotion-chasing Leicester City at Portman Road followed, but the game failed to live up to its pre-match billing and ended up in a hugely disappointing goalless draw. From a Town perspective, worse was to follow three days later when Watford arrived at Portman Road and left with a 2-1 win in the bag, putting a huge dent in Town's promotion ambitions. Again Hornets 'keeper David James produced a man-of-the-match performance.

Next up, Town and their supporters made the relatively short journey to the Abbey Stadium for the East Anglian derby against arch-rivals Cambridge United.

LINIGHAN'S SEASON IS OVER

For the first time in twelve games, John Lyall decided to change the team, bringing in Goddard and Zondervan to replace Johnson and Palmer. The strong wind again spoilt the match as a spectacle, but Town drew first blood just after the break and looked to be hanging on for a vital win only for a controversial second-half equaliser to give United a share of the spoils.

The goal came from a long throw that was comfortably held by Forrest only for Heathcote to impede the Town 'keeper forcing him to drop the ball allowing the United central-defender to back-heel the loose ball over the line.

Town had now slipped to third in the league, but as March drew to a close, consecutive home games against promotion rivals Derby County and Barnsley presented them with a great opportunity to make up lost ground.

The Rams were one of Division Two's big spenders having spent over £4 million in their efforts to clinch promotion, but they were soundly beaten by a rampant Town side that were two goals up after only 15 minutes. There were only two minutes on the clock when a fantastic through ball from Zondervan released Dozzell who raced clear to beat Sutton with a great finish.

On the quarter-hour mark, the Town striker added a second, heading home Thompson's corner in emphatic fashion. Derby came into the contest more in the second half and Simpson managed to pull a goal back eight minutes from time, but Town's defence held firm through to the final whistle.

The victory saw Town move into top spot in Division Two for the first time since the first month of the season and they consolidated their position three days later with a 2-0 victory over Barnsley at Portman Road, both goals coming from Chris Kiwomya either side of half-time.

Sadly, the victory came at a cost when skipper David Linighan was forced to leave the field with a serious knee injury that would ultimately keep him out of the team for the rest of the campaign.

DIVISION TWO

31 MARCH 1992		P	W	D	L	F	A	GD	P
1	Ipswich Town	38	20	10	8	58	39	19	70
2	Blackburn Rovers	39	19	9	11	59	42	17	66
3	Cambridge United	39	17	14	8	54	37	17	65
4	Charlton Athletic	39	18	8	13	48	43	5	62
5	Middlesbrough	35	17	10	8	43	29	14	61
6	Leicester City	37	17	8	12	48	44	4	59
7	Portsmouth	38	16	10	12	57	44	13	58
8	Derby County	38	17	7	14	53	45	8	58
9	Southend United	39	16	9	14	57	51	6	57
10	Swindon Town	38	15	11	12	63	51	12	56
11	Wolverhampton Wanderers	38	15	10	13	52	43	9	55
12	Barnsley	39	14	9	16	40	47	-7	51
13	Watford	39	14	8	17	40	43	-3	50
14	Millwall	38	14	8	16	54	62	-8	50
15	Tranmere Rovers	37	11	16	10	44	45	-1	49
16	Bristol Rovers	39	12	12	15	46	56	-10	48
17	Grimsby Town	38	12	10	16	44	55	-11	46
18	Newcastle United	40	11	13	16	58	72	-14	46
19	Bristol City	39	10	14	15	44	58	-14	44
20	Sunderland	36	12	7	17	48	51	-3	43
21	Brighton and Hove Albion	40	11	10	19	48	63	-15	43
22	Oxford United	38	11	8	19	55	60	-5	41
23	Plymouth Argyle	39	11	8	20	36	55	-19	41
24	Port Vale	40	9	13	18	37	51	-14	40

For their next game, a local derby away to Southend United, Phil Whelan was handed his first-team league debut, taking over the number six shirt in place of the side-lined Town skipper, with Jason Dozzell taking over the captaincy.

Southend were still very much in contention for a play-off place and during the first half, Forrest was called upon to produce a number of excellent saves to keep them at bay.

However, just after the break Phil Whelan capped a dream day when he rose at the far post to head home Neil Thompson's corner.

With fifteen minutes remaining, Town had a great opportunity to make the game safe when Dozzell was brought down in the box, but the resulting penalty kick was blasted onto the bar by Wark.

PHIL WHELAN RACES TO CELEBRATE WITH THE FANS AFTER SCORING AT SOUTHEND

GOALMOUTH ACTION V WOLVES

To make matters worse, the home side immediately went down to the other end to grab an equaliser when Prior headed home after Forrest had misjudged a right-wing cross.

Amazingly, just when a vital victory appeared to have been snatched from their grasp, Town managed to produce a truly grand finale to win the game in the very last minute.

Kiwomya was the architect, releasing Thompson down the left with a great ball allowing the full-back to race clear before curling a tremendous right-foot shot into the corner of the net much to the joy of Town's travelling fans.

With two home games to come in the week that lay ahead, promotion now seemed to be very much within reach for John Lyall and his team. Wolverhampton Wanderers were the midweek visitors to Portman Road.

Boasting the strike partnership of Steve Bull and Andy Mutch, the Midlands side could not be taken lightly and the pair did have a number of decent opportunities during the first half, but were made to pay in the 58th minute when Whelan was again the hero, heading home a Thompson free-kick to give Town the lead.

The scoreline was a little harsh on the visitors who arguably had been the better side and they got their reward with five minutes remaining when Mutch levelled the scores. The drama had not ended there however, for in the final minute, the referee adjudged that Kiwomya had been brought down in the box.

Despite the protests from the angry Wolves players Whitton stepped up to drive the spot-kick into the net and clinch a victory that would take Town seven points clear at the top, surely an unassailable lead?

Town's next game was against relegation-threatened Newcastle United who brought with them an army of supporters that boosted the Portman Road attendance to just under 21,000. The game developed into a really thrilling encounter with Town twice coming from behind to finally win by the odd goal in five.

MICHAEL STOCKWELL

PLAYER PROFILE

DATE OF BIRTH:	**14 February 1965**
PLACE OF BIRTH:	**Chelmsford**
IPSWICH TOWN (ALL COMPS):	**610 Appearances · 44 Goals**
1991/92 (LEAGUE ONLY):	**46 Appearances · 2 Goals**

A veteran of over 600 appearances in the blue and white of Ipswich Town, midfielder Mick Stockwell progressed through the Ipswich Town youth system after arriving from Leyton Orient.

Stockwell received the perfect Christmas present from boss Bobby Ferguson in 1985 when he was handed his Town debut on Boxing Day. Stockwell replaced Alan Sunderland in Town's match away to Coventry City as a Mich DAvray goal gave the Blues all three points from their trip to Highfield Road.

The Essex-born midfielder, who could also fill in at right-back, became a regular face in the Town line-up for the following 14 seasons.

Stockwell was ever-present in Town's 1991/92 Second Division title-winning season and chipped in with two goals too. He had no problem in stepping up to the Premier League in 1992/93 and ended the campaign as Town's Player of the Season.

He won a second promotion with the Blues in 1999/2000 as Town toppled Barnsley in the play-offs to secure promotion back to the top flight.

Stockwell left Portman Road in the summer of 2000 and ended his career with Colchester United. He was inducted into the Ipswich Town Hall of Fame in 2013.

MICK STOCKWELL 1993/94

STEPHEN PALMER

PLAYER PROFILE

DATE OF BIRTH:	**31 March 1968**
PLACE OF BIRTH:	**Brighton**
IPSWICH TOWN (ALL COMPS):	**131 Appearances · 3 Goals**
1991/92 (LEAGUE ONLY):	**23 Appearances**

Spotted by Town when playing university football for Cambridge University AFC, Steve Palmer remains the only professional footballer of the modern era to be educated at Cambridge University.

A talented sportsman, Palmer once played first-class cricket for a Cambridge University side against Lancashire in 1987 before deciding football was his game and turning professional with Ipswich in 1989.

His Blues debut arrived in a League Cup tie at home to Tranmere Rovers on 19 September 1989 when he replaced Louie Donowa. The defender went on to make 111 league appearances for Town, 23 of which came in the memorable 1991/92 Second Division title-winning campaign.

A valuable member of the Town squad across the following there seasons in the Premier League, Palmer left Portman Road in 1995 when he completed a £135,000 transfer to Watford.

In total, his career saw him play over 500 league games having also served Queens Park Rangers and MK Dons after a successful six-year spell at Vicarage Road.

Peacock opened the scoring for the visitors in the 18th minute with a terrific shot from the edge of the box only for Town to draw level when Whitton netted from the penalty spot after Ranson had handled in the box. Nevertheless, before the break, the Magpies were in front again with a brilliant solo goal from Peacock and for a long spell after the break it looked as though the points would be heading back to Tyneside.

Then with just over twenty minutes left, John Wark came to Town's rescue, just as he had done so many times in his long and illustrious Portman Road career.

Racing into the box he met Thompson's right-wing corner to send a bullet-header screaming into the net. A few minutes later the home fans were in raptures as Kiwomya put Town in front from close-range after a great run and cross by substitute Palmer.

The visitors came back strongly in the closing stages, but Town's rearguard kept them at bay to clinch a vital win that took them ten points clear at the top. The Premier League, it seemed, was now within touching distance.

A 3-0 defeat at FA Cup finalists Sunderland a few days later put Town's promotion celebrations on hold, while hordes of supporters headed over to the west country for their next game against Bristol City at Ashton Gate to see if their heroes could finally clinch promotion.

Sadly, Town failed to hit anything like their best form and after goals from Rosenior and a young Andy Cole had given the home side the lead, Town's only reply was a second-half Steve Whitton penalty after Kiwomya had been brought down.

The following week a crowd of over 22,000 packed Portman Road for the visit of lowly Grimsby Town, hoping that Ipswich Town would finally pick up the victory that would clinch automatic promotion. Before the game, John Wark was presented with his Players' Player of the Year trophy, but the game itself was a huge disappointment and ended goalless meaning that Town still needed one point from their last two games.

JOHN WARK EQUALISES AGAINST THE MAGPIES

PHIL WHELAN BEATS DAVID KELLY IN THE AIR

TOWN
TEN POINTS
CLEAR

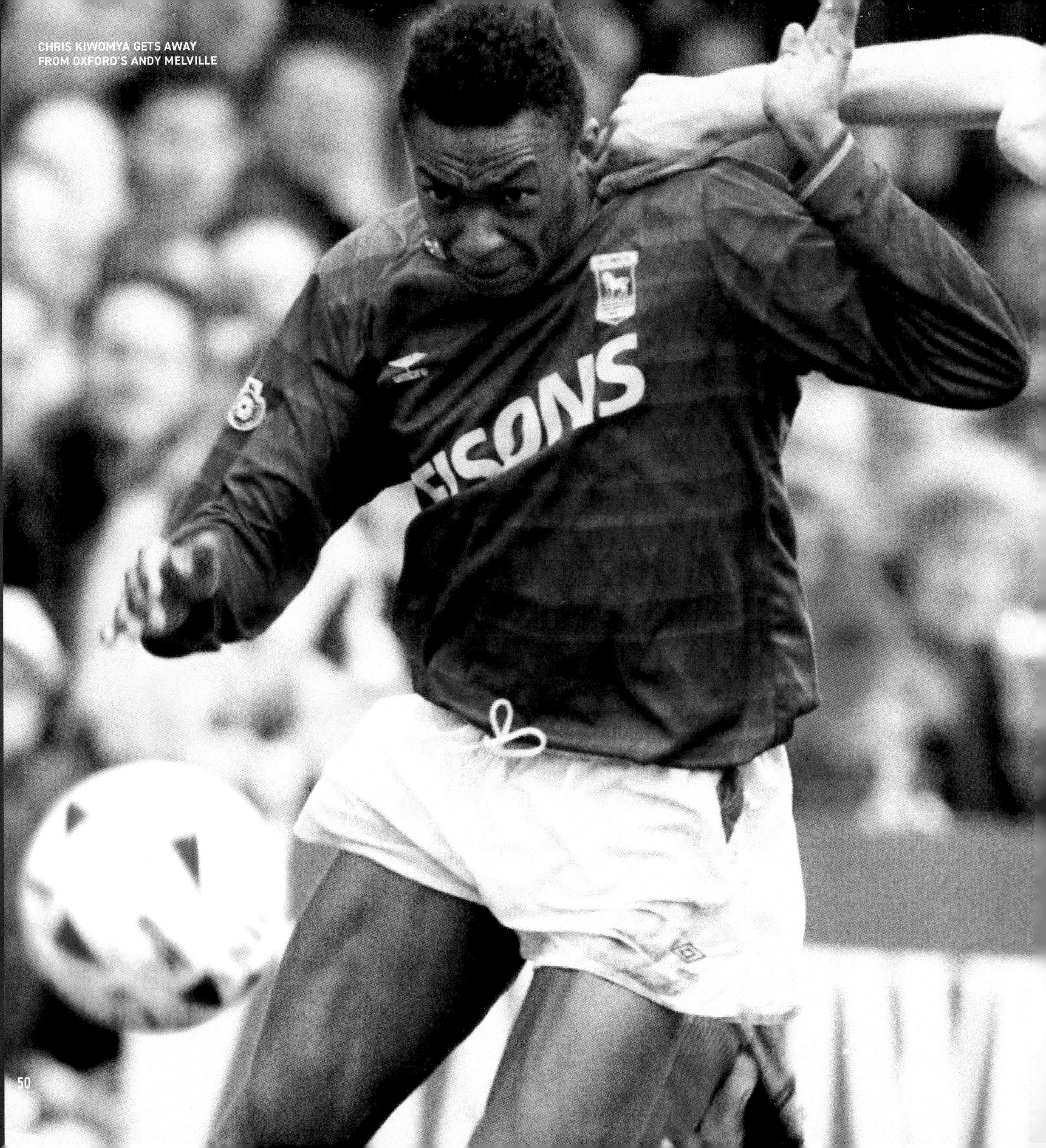

CHRIS KIWOMYA GETS AWAY
FROM OXFORD'S ANDY MELVILLE

The first of those was a visit to Oxford United and thousands of Town supporters invaded the varsity city, hoping to see their team finally claim their place in the Premier League. They did not get off to the best of starts when Magilton gave the home side the lead after only seven minutes, but they were level within two minutes when Johnson headed home Whitton's free-kick at the far post sparking huge celebrations among the massed ranks of their supporters.

That was the end of the scoring and at the final whistle jubilant Town fans were on the pitch in their hundreds to congratulate their heroes. The point meant that promotion had been achieved, but results elsewhere also meant that they had also won the Second Division title and passage to the Premier League.

DIVISION TWO

	30 APRIL 1992	P	W	D	L	F	A	GD	P
1	Ipswich Town	45	23	12	10	67	49	18	81
2	Middlesbrough	45	22	11	12	56	40	16	77
3	Leicester City	45	23	8	14	61	53	8	77
4	Derby County	45	22	9	14	67	50	17	75
5	Cambridge United	45	19	16	10	63	45	18	73
6	Blackburn Rovers	45	20	11	14	67	52	15	71
7	Charlton Athletic	45	20	11	14	54	47	7	71
8	Swindon Town	45	18	15	12	68	53	15	69
9	Portsmouth	45	18	12	15	63	51	12	66
10	Wolverhampton Wanderers	45	18	10	17	60	52	8	64
11	Southend United	45	17	11	17	63	61	2	62
12	Watford	45	17	11	17	46	46	0	62
13	Tranmere Rovers	45	14	19	12	55	54	1	61
14	Bristol Rovers	45	15	14	16	59	63	-4	59
15	Barnsley	45	16	11	18	46	55	-9	59
16	Millwall	45	16	10	19	62	71	-9	58
17	Bristol City	45	13	15	17	53	66	-13	54
18	Sunderland	45	14	10	21	59	63	-4	52
19	Grimsby Town	45	13	11	21	46	62	-16	50
20	Newcastle United	45	12	13	20	64	83	-19	49
21	Plymouth Argyle	45	13	9	23	41	61	-20	48
22	Oxford United	45	12	11	22	64	72	-8	47
23	Brighton and Hove Albion	45	12	11	22	55	74	-19	47
24	Port Vale	45	10	15	20	42	58	-16	45

The joyous celebrations continued a week later when an all-ticket crowd of over 26,000 packed Portman Road for the visit of Brighton and Hove Albion.

Before the game, injured skipper, David Linighan was presented with the Second Division Championship trophy while Chairman John Kerr was handed a cheque for £50,000 for winning the Division Two championship and John Lyall was presented with a magnum of champagne. Other presentations included Mick Stockwell picking up the Fisons Player of the Year award and John Wark who was voted Supporters Player of the Year.

Whilst the result was now academic, Town signed off in style with a terrific 3-1 victory. They opened the scoring after eight minutes when Whitton netted his fourth penalty of the season after Kiwomya had been upended in the box. Johnson doubled their advantage just before the break with a great shot from the edge of the box. Almost immediately however, Meade grabbed a consolation goal for the visitors, but Town finally sealed the victory eight minutes from time when Whitton grabbed his second of the game, a spectacular diving header from Thompson's corner.

At the final whistle, fans poured onto the pitch to mob their heroes before the players climbed up to the front of the director's box to join in the celebrations that continued 24 hours later when an open-topped bus carrying players and officials inched its way through the massed ranks of supporters prior to a civic reception at Cornhill.

It had been a magnificent finale to what had been a truly unbelievable campaign for John Lyall and his players. Amazingly, Ipswich Town had now won their place as inaugural members of the Premier League, a league that would soon become without doubt the greatest league in world club football.

With typical modesty, John Lyall gave all of the credit for his team's magnificent achievement to everyone associated with Ipswich Town Football Club:

"When I came to the club two years ago, I did not in all honesty expect success quite so quickly, but such has been the attitude of everyone here, that we have achieved something very positive. There are so many people to thank, but I must start with the players who have done it. We can all be behind them one hundred per cent, but if they don't respond in the right way, you do not get success. There has been a group of eighteen or so players who have been involved and they have put the club in the Premier League. They all deserve great praise".

"Ipswich is a special club and I have had two extremely happy years here. From the day I arrived, I have had great help from everyone, from the two chairmen Mr Patrick Cobbold and Mr John Kerr and the Board of Directors, the people who work in the offices and at the ground and from the supporters".

"My coaching and medical staff have done a great job. People won't fully realise how much work has been done on the training ground, but there have been countless hours spent out there".

DAVID LINIGHAN HOLDS ALOFT THE SECOND DIVISION CHAMPIONS TROPHY

"I am delighted that it has all come to fruition. It is an analysis of life that the harder you work the more you get out of it. That has always been my philosophy of football. It has not always worked. Last year we had our critics who perhaps thought that the club was going nowhere. People like myself knew that we were trying to do things and we had the patience to see it through".

"Nothing comes easy in football and there have been days during the season when things have not worked out. But if you look at us over the season, I think that fairly and justifiably we deserve to be champions".

SIMON MILTON, JASON DOZZELL, CHRIS KIWOMYA
AND JOHN WARK CELEBRATE WITH THE TROPHY

CHRIS KIWOMYA

DIVISION TWO								
2 MAY 1992	P	W	D	L	F	A	GD	P
1 Ipswich Town	46	24	12	10	70	50	20	84
2 Middlesbrough	46	23	11	12	58	41	17	80
3 Derby County	46	23	9	14	69	51	18	78
4 Leicester City	46	23	8	15	62	55	7	77
5 Cambridge United	46	19	17	10	65	47	18	74
6 Blackburn Rovers	46	21	11	14	70	53	17	74
7 Charlton Athletic	46	20	11	15	54	48	6	71
8 Swindon Town	46	18	15	13	69	55	14	69
9 Portsmouth	46	19	12	15	65	51	14	69
10 Watford	46	18	11	17	51	48	3	65
11 Wolverhampton Wanderers	46	18	10	18	61	54	7	64
12 Southend United	46	17	11	18	63	63	0	62
13 Bristol Rovers	46	16	14	16	60	63	-3	62
14 Tranmere Rovers	46	14	19	13	56	56	0	61
15 Millwall	46	17	10	19	64	71	-7	61
16 Barnsley	46	16	11	19	46	57	-11	59
17 Bristol City	46	13	15	18	55	71	-16	54
18 Sunderland	46	14	11	21	61	65	-4	53
19 Grimsby Town	46	14	11	21	47	62	-15	53
20 Newcastle United	46	13	13	20	66	84	-18	52
21 Oxford United	46	13	11	22	66	73	-7	50
22 Plymouth Argyle	46	13	9	24	42	64	-22	48
23 Brighton and Hove Albion	46	12	11	23	56	77	-21	47
24 Port Vale	46	10	15	21	42	59	-17	45

NEIL THOMPSON

PLAYER PROFILE

DATE OF BIRTH:	**2 October 1963**
PLACE OF BIRTH:	**Beverley**
IPSWICH TOWN (ALL COMPS):	**246 Appearances · 23 Goals**
1991/92 (LEAGUE ONLY):	**45 Appearances · 6 Goals**

A shrewd £100,000 signing from Scarborough in the summer of 1989, left-back Neil Thompson made his Ipswich Town debut in a 3-1 Portman Road victory over Barnsley on the opening day of the 1989/90 season.

Thompson had already made a positive impression on Town fans a week earlier when he scored in Ipswich's 4-0 pre-season Hospital Cup victory over Norwich City. The Beverly-born full-back went on to play almost 250 games for Ipswich and was a firm fixture in the starting line-up in the first five of his seven seasons at Portman Road.

He missed just one 1991/92 league game, a 1-0 defeat away to Middlesbrough. An attacking full-back, Thompson loved to roam forward and support Town's attacking play and he scored six goals in the promotion-winning campaign.

A vital component of the title-winning side, Thompson was one of many Town players who swiftly adapted to life in the Premier League and he gave Town fans a perfect early Christmas gift when he scored the second to secure a 2-0 East Anglian derby victory over Norwich at Carrow Road on 21 December 1992.

Thompson moved on to Barnsley in 1996 and also plied his trade at Oldham Athletic (loan), York City, Scarborough and Boston United. He is currently coaching at League One rivals Sheffield Wednesday.

STEPHEN WHITTON 1992/93

STEPHEN WHITTON

PLAYER PROFILE	
DATE OF BIRTH:	**4 December 1960**
PLACE OF BIRTH:	**East Ham, London**
IPSWICH TOWN (ALL COMPS):	**109 Appearances · 19 Goals**
1991/92 (LEAGUE ONLY):	**43 Appearances · 9 Goals**

Much-travelled striker Steve Whitton played a vital role in Ipswich Town's 1991/92 title triumph with nine goals from his 43 league appearances.

The London-born frontman began his career at Coventry City before being signed by John Lyall for West Ham United in 1983. After three years at Upton Park, Whitton joined Birmingham City and later Sheffield Wednesday but was reunited with Lyall when he joined Town in January 1991.

A powerful forward with an excellent understanding of those around him, and a good eye for goal, Whitton was part of an impressive forward line with Chris Kiwomya and Paul Goddard in 1991/92.

His first goal of the 1991/92 season helped seal a 2-1 home victory over Oxford United and he ended the campaign in style with a brace as Town defeated Brighton & Hove Albion 3-1 on a day of mass celebration at Portman Road.

He plied his trade with Town in the Premier League over the next two seasons before ending his playing career with a stint at Colchester United - a club where he later held the role of assistant manager.

WE ARE THE CHAMPIONS

60

THE ROUTE TO THE 1991/92 DIVISION TWO TITLE

BRISTOL ROVERS 3

Stewart, White 2.

IPSWICH TOWN 3

Dozzell, Goddard, Stockwell.

DATE: Saturday 17 August 1991

VENUE: Twerton Park   **ATTENDANCE:** 6,444

TOWN TEAM: Forrest, Yallop, Thompson, Zondervan, Gayle, Humes, Stockwell, Goddard, Johnson, Dozzell, Kiwomya.
SUB USED: Lowe.

IPSWICH TOWN 2

Kiwomya, Thompson (pen).

PORT VALE 1

Walker (pen).

DATE: Tuesday 20 August 1991

VENUE: Portman Road   **ATTENDANCE:** 8,937

TOWN TEAM: Forrest, Johnson, Thompson, Stockwell, Gayle, Humes, Zondervan, Goddard, Whitton, Dozzell, Kiwomya.
SUB USED: Yallop.

IPSWICH TOWN 2

Dozzell, Goddard.

MIDDLESBROUGH 1

Wilkinson.

DATE: Saturday 24 August 1991

VENUE: Portman Road   **ATTENDANCE:** 9,822

TOWN TEAM: Forrest, Johnson, Thompson, Stockwell, Gayle, Linighan, Zondervan, Goddard, Whitton, Dozzell, Kiwomya.
SUBS USED: Yallop, Lowe.

BLACKBURN ROVERS 1

Speedie.

IPSWICH TOWN 2

Kiwomya, Goddard.

DATE: Saturday 31 August 1991

VENUE: Ewood Park   **ATTENDANCE:** 8,898

TOWN TEAM: Forrest, Johnson, Thompson, Stockwell, Gayle, Linighan, Zondervan, Goddard, Whitton, Dozzell, Kiwomya.

IPSWICH TOWN 1

Kiwomya.

SWINDON TOWN 4

White, Calderwood, Taylor, Hazard.

DATE: Tuesday 3 September 1991

VENUE: Portman Road   **ATTENDANCE:** 11,002

TOWN TEAM: Forrest, Johnson, Thompson, Stockwell, Gayle, Linighan, Zondervan, Goddard, Whitton, Dozzell, Kiwomya.
SUBS USED: Lowe, Yallop.

IPSWICH TOWN 1

Thompson (pen).

SOUTHEND UNITED 0

DATE: Saturday 7 September 1991

VENUE: Portman Road   **ATTENDANCE:** 12,732

TOWN TEAM: Forrest, Johnson, Thompson, Stockwell, Humes, Linighan, Zondervan, Goddard, Whitton, Dozzell, Kiwomya.
SUB USED: Lowe.

BARNSLEY 1

Currie.

IPSWICH TOWN 0

DATE: Saturday 14 September 1991

VENUE: Oakwell   **ATTENDANCE:** 6,786

TOWN TEAM: Forrest, Johnson, Thompson, Stockwell, Humes, Linighan, Zondervan, Goddard, Whitton, Dozzell, Kiwomya.
SUBS USED: Lowe.

NEWCASTLE UNITED 1

Quinn (pen).

IPSWICH TOWN 1

Kiwomya.

DATE: Tuesday 17 September 1991

VENUE: St James' Park   **ATTENDANCE:** 16,336

TOWN TEAM: Forrest, Johnson, Thompson, Stockwell, Humes, Linighan, Zondervan, Goddard, Whitton, Dozzell, Kiwomya.
SUB USED: Yallop.

IPSWICH TOWN 4

Thompson, Linighan, Kiwomya, Goddard.

BRISTOL CITY 2

Allison, Smith.

DATE: Saturday 21 September 1991

VENUE: Portman Road   **ATTENDANCE:** 9,692

TOWN TEAM: Forrest, Johnson, Thompson, Stockwell, Yallop, Linighan, Zondervan, Goddard, Whitton, Dozzell, Kiwomya.
SUBS USED: Milton, Lowe.

GRIMSBY TOWN 1

Gilbert.

IPSWICH TOWN 2

Lowe, Johnson.

DATE: Saturday 28 September 1991

VENUE: Blundell Park   **ATTENDANCE:** 6,621

TOWN TEAM: Forrest, Johnson, Thompson, Stockwell, Yallop, Linighan, Lowe, Zondervan, Whitton, Dozzell, Kiwomya.
SUB USED: Wark.

IPSWICH TOWN 2

Milton, Whitton.

OXFORD UNITED 1

Magilton.

DATE: Saturday 5 October 1991

VENUE: Portman Road   **ATTENDANCE:** 9,922

TOWN TEAM: Forrest, Wark, Thompson, Stockwell, Yallop, Linighan, Lowe, Zondervan, Whitton, Milton, Kiwomya.

BRIGHTON & HOVE ALBION 2

Byrne, Chivers.

IPSWICH TOWN 2

Milton, Dozzell.

DATE: Saturday 12 October 1991

VENUE: Goldstone Ground   **ATTENDANCE:** 9,010

TOWN TEAM: Forrest, Wark, Thompson, Stockwell, Zondervan, Linighan, Lowe, Milton, Whitton, Dozzell, Kiwomya.
SUB USED: Gregory.

IPSWICH TOWN 0

MILLWALL 0

DATE: Saturday 19 October 1991

VENUE: Portman Road   **ATTENDANCE:** 11,175

TOWN TEAM: Forrest, Yallop, Thompson, Stockwell, Wark, Linighan, Lowe, Zondervan, Whitton, Dozzell, Milton.
SUB USED: Edmonds.

PORTSMOUTH 1

Burns.

IPSWICH TOWN 1

Milton.

DATE: Saturday 26 October 1991

VENUE: Fratton Park   **ATTENDANCE:** 8,007

TOWN TEAM: Forrest, Yallop, Thompson, Stockwell, Wark, Linighan, Lowe, Zondervan, Whitton, Dozzell, Milton.
SUBS USED: Moncur, Johnson.

DARREN EDMONDS

DATE OF BIRTH:	**12 April 1971**
PLACE OF BIRTH:	**Watford**
IPSWICH TOWN (ALL COMPS):	**3 Appearances**
1991/92 (LEAGUE ONLY):	**2 Appearances**

Winger Darren Edmonds began his career as a youth player with Leeds United, but failed to progress to the first-team at Elland Road and joined Ipswich Town early in the 1991/92 campaign.

Darren made his Town debut when he came on as substitute in the 0-0 draw with Millwall at Portman Road, but made only two more first-team appearances, on both occasions coming off the bench.

His brief Portman Road career came to end during the 1992 close season when he moved into non-league football eventually serving Scarborough, Mossley and Halifax Town.

BRIAN GAYLE

PLAYER PROFILE

DATE OF BIRTH:	**6 March 1965**
PLACE OF BIRTH:	**Kingston upon Thames**
IPSWICH TOWN (ALL COMPS):	**62 Appearances · 4 Goals**
1991/92 (LEAGUE ONLY):	**5 Appearances**

A powerfully built, rugged central-defender, Brian Gayle first came to prominence in Wimbledon's 'Crazy Gang' team of the 1980s that lifted the FA Cup in 1988.

Unfortunately, a red card received in one of the earlier rounds cost Brian his place in the final, an epic victory over Liverpool that would go down as one of the biggest upsets in the history of the competition.

Soon afterwards, he left Plough Lane to join Manchester City in a £325,000 deal, but two years later after failing to settle at Maine Road, Ipswich moved in to clinch his signature for a similar fee.

Brian began the 1991/92 season wearing the number five shirt, but after only five appearances early in the campaign he was,

perhaps somewhat surprisingly, sold to Sheffield United for £750,000.

He spent five seasons with the Yorkshire club before dropping down to the lower leagues when he played for Exeter City, Rotherham United, Bristol Rovers, Shrewsbury Town and finally finishing his playing days at non-league Telford United.

ANTHONY HUMES

PLAYER PROFILE

DATE OF BIRTH:	**19 March 1966**
PLACE OF BIRTH:	**Blyth**
IPSWICH TOWN (ALL COMPS):	**140 Appearances · 12 Goals**
1991/92 (LEAGUE ONLY):	**5 Appearances**

Born in Blyth during England's World Cup winning year of 1966, defender Tony Humes began his career as an apprentice with Ipswich Town in the summer of 1982.

Humes swiftly progressed through the ranks at Portman Road and was rewarded with a first professional contract in July 1983. Following Town's relegation from the top flight in 1985/86, Humes made his professional debut when he replaced Mick Stockwell in a goalless draw away to Blackburn Rovers in November 1986.

He went on to make a further 27 first-team appearances in 1986/87 and established himself as a regular face in the first team during John Duncan's three-season tenure.

Humes suffered a broken arm against Newcastle United in the early stages of 1991/92 and that proved to be his final game for Ipswich.

After returning from injury, he joined Wrexham in March 1992. He made over 200 outings while at the Racecourse, many as captain, and after ending his playing career with the Red Dragons, he has since worked in the Ipswich Academy, managed Colchester United and is currently the U's Director of Football.

65

CHARLTON ATHLETIC 1
Gatting.

IPSWICH TOWN 1
Whitton.

DATE: Wednesday 30 October 1991

VENUE: Upton Park **ATTENDANCE:** 6,939

TOWN TEAM: Forrest, Yallop, Thompson, Stockwell, Wark, Linighan, Johnson, Moncur, Whitton, Dozzell, Milton.

LEICESTER CITY 2
Kitson, Oldfield.

IPSWICH TOWN 2
Wark, Johnson.

DATE: Saturday 2 November 1991

VENUE: Filbert Street **ATTENDANCE:** 11,331

TOWN TEAM: Forrest, Yallop, Thompson, Stockwell, Wark, Linighan, Lowe, Milton, Whitton, Dozzell, Kiwomya.

SUB USED: Johnson.

IPSWICH TOWN 0

SUNDERLAND 1
Armstrong.

DATE: Tuesday 5 November 1991

VENUE: Portman Road **ATTENDANCE:** 9,768

TOWN TEAM: Forrest, Yallop, Thompson, Stockwell, Wark, Linighan, Milton, Moncur, Whitton, Dozzell, Kiwomya.

SUBS USED: Johnson, Edmonds.

IPSWICH TOWN 1
Stockwell.

CAMBRIDGE UNITED 2
Rowett, Claridge.

DATE: Saturday 9 November 1991

VENUE: Portman Road **ATTENDANCE:** 20,586

TOWN TEAM: Forrest, Johnson, Thompson, Stockwell, Wark, Linighan, Milton, Moncur, Whitton, Dozzell, Kiwomya.

66 **SUB USED:** Yallop.

DERBY COUNTY 1
Davison.

IPSWICH TOWN 0

DATE: Saturday 16 November 1991

VENUE: Baseball Ground **ATTENDANCE:** 12,493

TOWN TEAM: Forrest, Youds, Thompson, Stockwell, Wark, Linighan, Lowe, Moncur, Johnson, Dozzell, Kiwomya.

SUB USED: Yallop.

WOLVERHAMPTON WANDERERS 1
Birch.

IPSWICH TOWN 2
Linighan, Dozzell.

DATE: Saturday 23 November 1991

VENUE: Molineux **ATTENDANCE:** 11,915

TOWN TEAM: Forrest, Johnson, Thompson, Stockwell, Wark, Linighan, Moncur, Goddard, Whitton, Dozzell, Kiwomya.

IPSWICH TOWN 4
Milton, Thompson, Linighan, Wark (pen).

TRANMERE ROVERS 0

DATE: Saturday 30 November 1991

VENUE: Portman Road **ATTENDANCE:** 11,072

TOWN TEAM: Forrest, Johnson, Thompson, Stockwell, Wark, Linighan, Milton, Palmer, Whitton, Dozzell, Kiwomya.

SUB USED: Lowe.

PLYMOUTH ARGYLE 1
Fiore.

IPSWICH TOWN 0

DATE: Saturday 7 December 1991

VENUE: Home Park **ATTENDANCE:** 4,986

TOWN TEAM: Forrest, Johnson, Thompson, Stockwell, Wark, Linighan, Milton, Palmer, Whitton, Dozzell, Kiwomya.

SUB USED: Yallop.

SWINDON TOWN 0

IPSWICH TOWN 0

DATE: Friday 20 December 1991

VENUE: County Ground **ATTENDANCE:** 7,404

TOWN TEAM: Forrest, Johnson, Thompson, Stockwell, Wark, Linighan, Milton, Palmer, Whitton, Dozzell, Kiwomya.

IPSWICH TOWN 2

Kiwomya 2.

CHARLTON ATHLETIC 0

DATE: Thursday 26 December 1991

VENUE: Portman Road **ATTENDANCE:** 13,826

TOWN TEAM: Forrest, Johnson, Thompson, Stockwell, Wark, Linighan, Pennyfather, Palmer, Milton, Dozzell, Kiwomya.

IPSWICH TOWN 2

Johnson, Dozzell.

BLACKBURN ROVERS 1

Wright.

DATE: Saturday 28 December 1991

VENUE: Portman Road **ATTENDANCE:** 17,657

TOWN TEAM: Forrest, Johnson, Thompson, Stockwell, Wark, Linighan, Milton, Palmer, Whitton, Dozzell, Kiwomya.
SUB USED: Pennyfather.

PORT VALE 1

Hughes.

IPSWICH TOWN 2

Kiwomya 2.

DATE: Wednesday 1 January 1992

VENUE: Vale Park **ATTENDANCE:** 8,075

TOWN TEAM: Forrest, Johnson, Thompson, Stockwell, Wark, Linighan, Milton, Palmer, Whitton, Dozzell, Kiwomya.

MIDDLESBROUGH 1

Payton.

IPSWICH TOWN 0

DATE: Saturday 11 January 1992

VENUE: Ayresome Park **ATTENDANCE:** 15,104

TOWN TEAM: Forrest, Johnson, Pennyfather, Stockwell, Wark, Linighan, Milton, Palmer, Whitton, Dozzell, Kiwomya.
SUB USED: Yallop.

IPSWICH TOWN 1

Milton.

BRISTOL ROVERS 0

DATE: Saturday 18 January 1992

VENUE: Portman Road **ATTENDANCE:** 10,435

TOWN TEAM: Forrest, Johnson, Thompson, Stockwell, Wark, Linighan, Milton, Palmer, Whitton, Dozzell, Kiwomya.
SUB USED: Zondervan.

MILLWALL 2

Rae, Kerr (pen).

IPSWICH TOWN 3

Dozzell, Thompson, Kiwomya.

DATE: Saturday 1 February 1992

VENUE: The Den **ATTENDANCE:** 8,847

TOWN TEAM: Forrest, Johnson, Thompson, Stockwell, Wark, Linighan, Milton, Palmer, Whitton, Dozzell, Kiwomya.
SUB USED: Zondervan.

IPSWICH TOWN 5

Dozzell 2, Kiwomya 2, Awford (og).

PORTSMOUTH 2

Anderton, Powell.

DATE: Saturday 8 February 1992

VENUE: Portman Road **ATTENDANCE:** 13,494

TOWN TEAM: Forrest, Johnson, Thompson, Stockwell, Wark, Linighan, Milton, Palmer, Whitton, Dozzell, Kiwomya.

LET'S GET
THIS PARTY
STARTED FISONS

69

TRANMERE ROVERS 0
IPSWICH TOWN 1
Milton.

DATE: Friday 21 February 1992
VENUE: Prenton Park **ATTENDANCE:** 9,161
TOWN TEAM: Forrest, Johnson, Thompson, Stockwell, Wark, Linighan, Milton, Palmer, Whitton, Dozzell, Kiwomya.
SUB USED: Goddard.

IPSWICH TOWN 2
Kiwomya, Whitton.
PLYMOUTH ARGYLE 0

DATE: Saturday 29 February 1992
VENUE: Portman Road **ATTENDANCE:** 12,852
TOWN TEAM: Forrest, Johnson, Thompson, Stockwell, Wark, Linighan, Milton, Palmer, Whitton, Dozzell, Kiwomya.
SUBS USED: Goddard, Zondervan.

WATFORD 0
IPSWICH TOWN 1
Whitton.

DATE: Saturday 7 March 1992
VENUE: Vicarage Road **ATTENDANCE:** 9,199
TOWN TEAM: Forrest, Johnson, Thompson, Stockwell, Wark, Linighan, Milton, Palmer, Whitton, Dozzell, Kiwomya.

IPSWICH TOWN 0
LEICESTER CITY 0

DATE: Saturday 14 March 1992
VENUE: Portman Road **ATTENDANCE:** 16,174
TOWN TEAM: Forrest, Johnson, Thompson, Stockwell, Wark, Linighan, Milton, Palmer, Whitton, Dozzell, Kiwomya.
SUB USED: Goddard.

IPSWICH TOWN 1
Dozzell.
WATFORD 2
Drysdale 2.

DATE: Tuesday 17 March 1992
VENUE: Portman Road **ATTENDANCE:** 12,484
TOWN TEAM: Forrest, Johnson, Thompson, Stockwell, Wark, Linighan, Milton, Palmer, Whitton, Dozzell, Kiwomya.
SUB USED: Goddard.

CAMBRIDGE UNITED 1
Heathcote.
IPSWICH TOWN 1
Milton.

DATE: Saturday 21 March 1992
VENUE: Abbey Stadium **ATTENDANCE:** 9,766
TOWN TEAM: Forrest, Zondervan, Thompson, Stockwell, Wark, Linighan, Milton, Goddard, Whitton, Dozzell, Kiwomya.

IPSWICH TOWN 2
Dozzell 2.
DERBY COUNTY 1
Simpson.

DATE: Saturday 28 March 1992
VENUE: Portman Road **ATTENDANCE:** 15,305
TOWN TEAM: Forrest, Zondervan, Thompson, Stockwell, Wark, Linighan, Milton, Goddard, Whitton, Dozzell, Kiwomya.
SUB USED: Johnson.

IPSWICH TOWN 2
Kiwomya 2.
BARNSLEY 0

DATE: Tuesday 31 March 1992
VENUE: Portman Road **ATTENDANCE:** 14,148
TOWN TEAM: Forrest, Zondervan, Thompson, Stockwell, Wark, Linighan, Milton, Goddard, Whitton, Dozzell, Kiwomya.
SUBS USED: Johnson, Palmer.

SOUTHEND UNITED 1
Prior.
IPSWICH TOWN 2
Whelan, Thompson.

DATE: Saturday 4 April 1992

VENUE: Roots Hall   **ATTENDANCE:** 10,003

TOWN TEAM: Forrest, Zondervan, Thompson, Stockwell, Wark, Whelan, Milton, Goddard, Whitton, Dozzell, Kiwomya.
SUBS USED: Palmer, Johnson.

IPSWICH TOWN 2
Whelan, Whitton (pen).
WOLVERHAMPTON WANDERERS 1
Mutch.

DATE: Tuesday 7 April 1992

VENUE: Portman Road   **ATTENDANCE:** 17,379

TOWN TEAM: Forrest, Zondervan, Thompson, Stockwell, Wark, Whelan, Milton, Goddard, Whitton, Dozzell, Kiwomya.
SUBS USED: Palmer, Johnson.

IPSWICH TOWN 3
Whitton (pen), Wark, Kiwomya.
NEWCASTLE UNITED 2
Peacock 2.

DATE: Saturday 11 April 1992

VENUE: Portman Road   **ATTENDANCE:** 20,673

TOWN TEAM: Forrest, Zondervan, Thompson, Stockwell, Wark, Whelan, Milton, Goddard, Whitton, Dozzell, Kiwomya.
SUBS USED: Palmer, Johnson.

SUNDERLAND 3
Goodman 2, Rush.
IPSWICH TOWN 0

DATE: Tuesday 14 April 1992

VENUE: Roker Park   **ATTENDANCE:** 22,131

TOWN TEAM: Forrest, Zondervan, Thompson, Stockwell, Wark, Whelan, Johnson, Palmer, Whitton, Dozzell, Kiwomya.
SUB USED: Milton.

BRISTOL CITY 2
Rosenior, Cole.
IPSWICH TOWN 1
Whitton (pen).

DATE: Saturday 18 April 1992

VENUE: Ashton Gate   **ATTENDANCE:** 16,931

TOWN TEAM: Forrest, Zondervan, Thompson, Stockwell, Wark, Whelan, Milton, Goddard, Whitton, Dozzell, Kiwomya.
SUBS USED: Palmer, Johnson.

IPSWICH TOWN 0
GRIMSBY TOWN 0

DATE: Tuesday 21 April 1992

VENUE: Portman Road   **ATTENDANCE:** 22,393

TOWN TEAM: Forrest, Zondervan, Thompson, Stockwell, Wark, Whelan, Milton, Johnson, Whitton, Dozzell, Kiwomya.
SUBS USED: Palmer, Goddard.

OXFORD UNITED 1
Magilton.
IPSWICH TOWN 1
Johnson.

DATE: Saturday 25 April 1992

VENUE: Manor Ground   **ATTENDANCE:** 10,525

TOWN TEAM: Forrest, Zondervan, Thompson, Stockwell, Wark, Whelan, Johnson, Goddard, Whitton, Dozzell, Kiwomya.

IPSWICH TOWN 3
Whitton 2 (1 pen), Johnson.
BRIGHTON & HOVE ALBION 1
Meade.

DATE: Saturday 2 May 1992

VENUE: Portman Road   **ATTENDANCE:** 26,803

TOWN TEAM: Forrest, Zondervan, Thompson, Stockwell, Wark, Whelan, Johnson, Goddard, Whitton, Dozzell, Kiwomya.
SUBS USED: Palmer, Milton.

PREMIER LEAGUE
HERE WE COME

" OUTSIDE OF SC F